Therapeutic Play Activities
for Hospitalized Children

Therapeutic Play Activities for Hospitalized Children

Robyn Hart, MEd, CCLS
Manager, Child Life Services,
Rush-Presbyterian-St. Luke's Medical Center,
Chicago, Illinois

Patricia L. Mather, PhD
Licensed Psychologist in Private Practice,
Arlington Heights, Illinois

Jeanne F. Slack, RN, DNSc
Associate Chairperson, Rush-Presbyterian-St. Luke's
Medical Center, Department of Maternal-Child Nursing,
Chicago, Illinois

Marcia A. Powell, MA, CTRS
Former Child Life Coordinator,
Mount Sinai Hospital Medical Center,
Chicago, Illinois

*with **48** illustrations*

Mosby
Year Book

St. Louis   Baltimore   Boston   Chicago   London   Philadelphia   Sydney   Toronto

**Mosby
Year Book**

Dedicated to Publishing Excellence

Senior Editor: Linda L. Duncan
Developmental Editor: Teri Merchant
Project Manager: Karen Edwards
Senior Production Editor: Gail Brower
Designer: David Zielinski
Illustrator: Kristen Wienandt
Photographers: Bill and Susan Richert

Printed in the United States of America.

Mosby–Year Book, Inc.
11830 Westline Industrial Drive
St. Louis, MO 63146

Library of Congress Cataloging in Publication Data

Therapeutic play activities for hospitalized children / Robyn Hart . . .
[et al.].
    p.   cm.
    Includes index.
    ISBN 0-8016-1636-0
    1. Children—Hospital care—Psychological aspects.   2. Teenagers—
Hospital care—Psychological aspects.   3. Play therapy.
4. Recreational therapy for children.   5. Recreational therapy for
teenagers.   I. Hart, Robyn.
    [DNLM: 1. Adolescent, Hospitalized—psychology.   2. Child,
Hospitalized—psychology.   3. Play Therapy—in adolescence.   4. Play
Therapy—in infancy & childhood.   WS 105.5.H7 T398]
RJ242.T48   1992
362.1'9892—dc20
DNLM/DLC   91-42357
for Library of Congress   CIP

92 93 94 95 96 CL/VH 9 8 7 6 5 4 3 2 1

To
Claire Jacobs
for support and guidance

PREFACE

Optimal care for sick children and adolescents involves more than meeting their physical needs; psychosocial needs are also important. Comprehensive care promotes adaptation and continued growth during the health care experience. Support to both the child and family are integral components in this process. Opportunities for play, learning, self-expression, peer interactions, and family involvement help the child or adolescent adapt and cope with illness.

Working in a pediatric unit and attempting to anticipate and provide for the needs of our patients, we constantly sought therapeutic exercises and activities that would conquer children's fear, improve their self-esteem, establish familiarity with procedures and surroundings, and generally care for the psychosocial as well as the medical needs of our patients.

This handbook contains activities that promote the psychosocial care for children and adolescents in a variety of health care settings. Chapter 1 contains an overview of the theoretical rationale for the book and a description of the different types of play intervention available to health care professionals and families. This chapter also presents the cultural, familial, and other variables affecting therapeutic play activities. Safety precautions for the use of play materials conclude the chapter.

Chapters 2 through 13 contain activities grouped to address specific psychosocial goals. Each chapter introduction contains background information explaining the rationale for activities, special considerations for conducting the activities, and the activity goals. Each activity identifies instructions important for its use:

- Age group: the range of ages for which the activity is most appropriate.
- Patient/staff ratio: maximum number of children per staff for conducting the activity.
- Approximate length of time: the amount of time to plan for the activity
- Therapeutic rationale: the means for evaluating the outcomes of play interventions; they define what behaviors to observe while the children or adolescents do the activities.
- Precautions and restrictions: safety information about materials; categories of children who should not participate in the activity.
- Required skills: developmental abilities necessary for the activity.
- Equipment: materials needed for the activity.
- Implementation: specific directions for doing the activity.

Variations are given for some activities.

This information will help professionals select the most appropriate activities for meeting specific treatment goals and enable the user to effectively use time and materials to meet the psychosocial needs of individuals or groups.

Acknowledgments
We thank Ann Wildblood for her contributions to this book and thank Felicia Nugent for typing the manuscript.

Robyn Hart
Patricia L. Mather
Jeanne F. Slack
Marcia A. Powell

CONTENTS

C H A P T E R
1

OVERVIEW OF
THERAPEUTIC PLAY

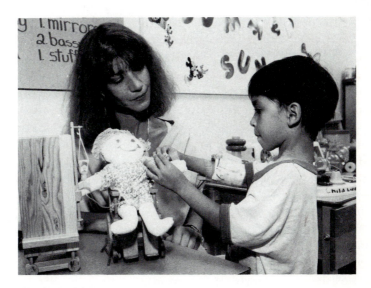

Fig.1-1

CHILDREN'S REACTIONS TO HEALTH CARE EXPERIENCES

A large body of theoretical and research literature describing the psychosocial needs of children and adolescents receiving health care exists in medical, nursing, child life, and other related publications. The purpose of this overview is not to review this literature in depth but to describe the major resources that form the theoretical framework for the activities in this book.

The effects of hospitalization and other health care experiences on children and adolescents have concerned professionals for many years. Vernon, Foley, Sipowicz, and Schulman (1965) reviewed research before 1965, with subsequent studies reviewed by Thompson (1985). Research shows that emotional distress in children is common during health care experiences and afterward. Long-term negative sequelae lasting from several weeks or months through adolescence may occur. Responses of the children vary from overt active responses (e.g., crying, clinging to parents, resistance to treatment, and destructive behavior) to passive responses (e.g., excessive sleeping, decreased communication, decreased activity, and decreased eating). Regressive behavior, or the return to earlier behaviors typical of a younger child, is also possible (Thompson & Stanford, 1981). Behavioral disturbances and learning problems in adolescents are associated with early and repeated hospitalizations (Douglas, 1975; Quinton & Rutter, 1976).

Recent investigation focuses on children's and adolescents' reactions to specific settings (e.g., emergency departments, intensive care units, home care) and various types of chronic conditions. The research confirms that reactions to stress occur in various settings by different types of sick children and adolescents (Alcock et al, 1984, 1985; Featherstone, 1981; Green, 1983; Magrab, 1985; Perrin & Gerrity, 1984; Willis, Elliott & Jay, 1982). Reactions vary according to individual differences, but all fall into the categories of active, passive, or regressive behaviors.

RESEARCH ON PSYCHOSOCIAL INTERVENTIONS

Early classic research (Prugh et al, 1953; Skipper & Leonard, 1968) indicates that psychological preparation for children and families, frequent parent visitation, and opportunities for play are associated with better adjustment during and after hospitalization. Recent evaluation research confirms their early findings: these interventions produce significant improvements. Several studies examine play and child life programming on a small scale (Carson, Jenkins & Stout, 1985; Clatworthy, 1981), with the most recent evidence coming from a major research project by Wolfer and his colleagues (Gaynard et al, 1990; Wolfer et al, 1988). This project looks at psychosocial programming for children hospitalized on inpatient units for various reasons and for differing lengths of time. Additional research shows interventions also work in other settings, specifically the emergency department (Alcock, Berthiaume & Clarke, 1984; Alcock et al, 1985) and the intensive care unit (Cataldo et al, 1979; Pearson et al, 1980). Both descriptive and research articles citing the value of play in doctors' waiting rooms, admissions areas, and other outpatient settings are also available (Alcock, Goodman et al, 1985; Williams & Powell, 1980; Wilson B, Hausslein, & McCormick, 1982; Wilson JM, 1988). Additional literature describes the use of psychosocial interventions with children having chronic conditions (Brill et al, 1987; McLane, 1986).

DEVELOPMENTAL THEORY AND THERAPEUTIC PLAY

Play is one of the most powerful and effective means of stress reduction for children (Petrillo & Sanger, 1981). Various psychodynamic, developmental, and cognitive theories address why this is so. Psychoanalytic theorists postulate that play is a means through which children act out unpleasant experiences and minimize resulting negative psychological impact (Freud, 1955, [vol 18]; Winnicott, 1965). Erikson (1950) suggests that in play, fantasy and reality meet, allowing fears and conflicts to be confronted and conquered. Through this process the child grows closer to psychological maturity. Piaget and Sponseller (Piaget, 1962; Sponseller, 1974) both state that play is the medium for learning about the world and how to interact with it. Oremland (1988) concludes that play promotes mastery of developmental and critical experiences and involves becoming active in situations in which the child is otherwise passive. Bolig, Fernie, and Klein (1986) note that play can help increase the internal locus of control of a pediatric patient.

Some professionals disagree on the definition of play as well as the amount of structure and involvement of the adult in this process. Bolig (1984, 1988, 1990) and her associates (Bolig, Fernie & Klein, 1986) note that play is a complex entity that is difficult to define. Play can mean either all the activities a child does or just those voluntary activities in which the child is intrinsically motivated, process-focused, pleasurably involved, and in an "as if" or pretend state. Play researchers tend to agree with the second definition. These voluntary activities are organism dominated rather than object dominated, unique, unpredictable, and active (either motorically or cognitively).

Gibbons and Boren (1985) describe three types of play beneficial for stress reduction. (1) **Recreational play** is spontaneous, unstructured play. It occurs naturally, and its content and form are affected by the developmental level of the child. (2) **Therapeutic play** occurs when an adult structures the activity for a specific purpose. It can be preparatory or cathartic. (3) Finally, **play therapy** involves interpreting children's play and recommending appropriate interventions. In this type of play, skilled therapists use play to help children understand their own behavior and change those behaviors that are inappropriate.

DelPo and Frick (1988) use the phrase "play as therapeutic modality" to describe adults' purposeful use of any type of play to facilitate communication with children. Play allows children to express thoughts and feelings, assimilate reality, resolve internal conflicts, achieve mastery, and cope effectively. It provides a vehicle for a child's self-expression and is a way in which children and adults can communicate. DelPo and Frick identify two types of therapeutic play interventions: directed therapeutic play and nondirected therapeutic play. In directed therapeutic play the adult is more active and predetermines the theme and content of the play experience. Nondirected therapeutic play is that initiated by the child, i.e., the child takes on an active role, while the adult is a participant-observer. DelPo and Frick note that although the methods and conceptual bases for both types of therapeutic play differ, the goals are the same: to provide experiences through which

the child can resolve internal conflicts and achieve mastery over difficult life experiences. Both types of play are important components of a comprehensive psychosocial approach to working with sick children. Schaefer (1976) states that health care professionals must have a broad view of all types of play to work effectively with children.

This handbook presents a variety of activities, some more structured than others. In general, they are directed therapeutic activities, but some can also be offered as an available activity in a nondirected playroom situation. Children and adolescents have choices within the parameters of an activity, depending on the adult's attitudes and responses.

FAMILIAL VARIABLES

The family is a potential source of support for the child and a link to the outside world. Ideally parents or other family members are intermediaries with members of the health care system and serve as advocates for their child's needs. They are important members of the health care team who help their child adapt and cope with illness.

The role of families in health care today differs from what it was 50 years ago (Johnson, 1990). Professionals now try to recognize families as experts to be consulted about the kind of support they need in assisting their sick child.

Johnson acknowledges that today's families are different than they were 50 years ago:

- There are more single-parent families.
- More mothers work.
- More children are born to adolescent and older mothers.
- Poverty is more prevalent.

There are also more dysfunctional families with addictions (Arneson, Triplett, Schweer & Snider, 1983). Health care professionals must be alert to the conditions within a family so that they can enable and empower them to deal more effectively with a health care experience (Dunst et al, 1988). The proposed model for this process is family-centered care, described by Johnson as (1990, p. 237):

- Recognizing that the family is the constant in a child's life, while the services systems and personnel within those systems fluctuate.

- Facilitating parent/professional collaboration at all levels of health care.
- Honoring the racial, ethnic, cultural, and socioeconomic diversity of families.
- Recognizing family strengths and individuality and respecting different methods of coping.
- Sharing with parents, on a continuing basis and in a supportive manner, complete and unbiased information.
- Encouraging and facilitating family-to-family support and networking.
- Understanding and incorporating the developmental needs of infants, children, and adolescents and their families into health care systems.
- Implementing comprehensive policies and programs that provide emotional and financial support to meet the needs of families.
- Designing accessible health care systems that are flexible, culturally competent, and responsive to family-identified needs.

Therapeutic play experiences are an integral part of family-centered care. Professionals and family members share activities with each other and participate in them. This participation promotes parent/professional collaboration and recognizes that families are constant in a child's life although the health care system is not. Professionals choose activities that reflect racial, ethnic, and cultural diversity to honor these aspects of children's backgrounds. Therapeutic play activities help the health care professional identify family strengths, individuality, and coping methods. During the activity the professional can provide information and model methods for helping children more effectively. Some programs encourage parents to be involved in group activities that can promote family-to-family networking via the same techniques used in therapeutic play activities with groups of children (Ritter & Klinzing, 1980).

CULTURAL VARIABLES

Many good references describe health care considerations when working with children from various cultural backgrounds, e.g., Asian (Abu-Saad, 1984; Manio & Hall, 1987; West, 1983), black (Powell, 1983), Hispanic (da Silva, 1984; Pilon & Smith, 1985), and native American (van

Breda, 1989). Although each culture differs, important components to consider when working with a family from a different culture include the following factors (Niederhauser, 1989):

- Religion—the relationship between religion, spirituality, and health varies across cultures. In some communities illness is viewed as punishment for misdeeds.
- Education and life views—educational background of family members varies according to culture, which can affect individuals' styles of learning. Life views affect the way family members view the present and future. It can also affect family values toward children and adolescents.
- Communication—cultures vary in their forms and styles of communication (e.g., oral vs written, indirect vs direct). The way in which information is perceived and understood can also reflect cultural differences.
- Time and personal space issues—some cultures revolve around time and deadlines, while others are more flexible. Personal space issues determine the amount of physical contact and distance that exists between individuals.
- Health and illness beliefs—for some cultures, health is primarily the absence of disease; it does not refer to preventive or mental health.
- Family practices—the roles of family members differ across cultures. Childrearing practices, attitudes toward women, and mothering may reflect cultural attitudes and training.

Health care professionals need to examine their own cultural values and consider how their views may differ from their patients' views. By objectively comparing their own culture with that of their patients, the health care professional learns to interact more effectively with families to understand and meet their needs.

ADAPTATION AND COPING WITH ILLNESS

Despite the stress that children undergo during illness, some children are resilient to the experience and adapt effectively to it (Bolig & Weddle, 1988; Burke, 1986). The premise of this handbook is that therapeutic play activities are an essential component of psychosocial programming to enhance children's ability to adapt and grow during an illness. The activities are useful in a variety of settings (e.g. home, outpatient and inpatient settings, skilled care facilities) with children of different familial and cultural backgrounds who have a variety of acute or chronic illnesses.

MAINTAINING A SAFE ENVIRONMENT AND ENSURING SAFE USE OF MATERIALS

The following guidelines are provided to ensure a safe environment for the child participating in therapeutic activities.

1. Children are naturally curious and learn from their senses of touch, taste, sight, hearing, and smell; therefore, a safe but stimulating environment with appropriate limits and supervision must be provided.
2. A child's developmental level can contribute to an increased tendency for an accident or injury. For example:
   a. Infants and toddlers use mouthing behaviors to explore. This behavior can lead to the ingestion of unsafe materials or injury from sharp objects.
   b. Toddlers often run with small toys or objects in their mouths. Caution should be used with any materials that could lead to choking.
   c. Children in middle or late childhood are more at risk for ingesting materials used in play or craft activities.
3. The child's developmental level should be evaluated to be sure that no discrepancy exists between developmental skill level and the child's ability to manipulate materials for the therapeutic activities.
4. Children with special needs:
   a. A child with a hearing or vision disability may require extra supervision during some therapeutic activities.
   b. A child who is hyperactive or has an attention deficit disorder may be excessively stimulated by some of the therapeutic activities. The child with a short attention span may be unable to follow directions or may react diffusely to

stimuli. Adjusting the amount of stimulation in the activities may be necessary.
   c. Children with known medical problems such as seizures, diabetes mellitus, asthma, and cystic fibrosis can be at a greater risk for injury during more vigorous activities. Permission for a child with a medical problem to participate in the therapeutic activities should be obtained. Some activities may have to be modified to reduce the risk of injury or aggravation to an existing health problem.
5. When selecting toys for therapeutic activities, the following principles should be considered.
   a. Follow all age recommendations and information concerning the safe use of the toys and materials.
   b. Toys or materials with sharp edges or points and small loose parts should not be used. Any objects that can be propelled must be used with close supervision.
   c. Toys with flexible joints can catch a child's finger.
   d. Only nontoxic materials should be used for young children.
   e. Infant-teething toys should be unbreakable and not contain liquid. Even a minute crack can allow bacterial growth in the liquid.
   f. Therapeutic activities involving the use of heating elements and electrical or chemical materials should be used with children more than 8 years old.
6. When selecting and using materials for therapeutic activities, the following guidelines to ensure child safety should be considered.
   a. *Balloons*—Balloons should be kept out of the reach of children under 3 years of age or those children who tend to put objects in their mouths. If a child were to have a balloon in his mouth and it popped, a piece of the balloon could be aspirated into the airway when the child suddenly inhales as a reflex response to the sudden event. The piece of balloon can block air passageways, causing hy-

poxia and even death. Children allowed to play with balloons require supervision.

b. *Glitter*—Glitter should be used only with children old enough to follow directions consistently. Glitter should not be used with children who may put fingers in their mouths or rub their eyes while working with glitter because it may be transferred from fingers to mouth or eyes. Children using glitter require supervision. Any observed or suspected problems should be reported promptly to the patient's nurse or physician.

c. *Glue/paste*—Glue and paste used with young children or with a child who is developmentally delayed should be nontoxic. Older children may be competent to work with other substances, such as for models. Consider also that strong odors of adhesive materials can be nauseating for certain sensitive individuals, such as postoperative patients or patients receiving chemotherapy. Any observed or suspected ingestion should be re-

ported promptly to the patient's nurse or physician.

d. *Markers*—Markers used with young children or a child who is developmentally delayed should be nontoxic. Consider also that some markers emit odors and may be nauseating for certain sensitive individuals, i.e., children in early postoperative phase or who are receiving chemotherapy. Any observed or suspected ingestion of these chemicals should be reported promptly to the patient's nurse or physician.

e. *Needles*—Using disposable needles ensures that needles are not reused by another child. Follow your institution's guidelines for disposal of needles (usually special containers are used). Precautions with needles or sharps are necessary to prevent injury to both the child and staff member(s).

f. *Scissors*—In any activities requiring the use of scissors, the participant should be taught the proper use of the scissors; for children less than 7, blunt scissors should be used.

REFERENCES

Abu-Saad, H. (1984). Cultural components of pain: The Asian-American child. *Children's Health Care, 13* (1), 11-14.

Alcock, D., Berthiaume, S., & Clarke, A. (1984). Child life intervention in the emergency department. *Children's Health Care, 12* (3), 130-136.

Alcock, D., Feldman, W., Goodman, J., McGrath, P., & Park, J. (1985). Evaluation of child life emergency department suturing. *Pediatric Emergency Care, 1,* 111-115.

Alcock, D., Goodman, J., Feldman, W., McGrath, P.J., Park, M., & Cappelli, M. (1985). Environment and waiting behaviors in emergency waiting areas. *Children's Health Care, 13* (4), 174-180.

Arneson, S.W., Triplett, J.L., Schweer, K.D., & Snider, B.C. (1983). Children of alcoholic parents: Identification and intervention. *Children's Health Care, 11* (3), 107-112.

Bolig, R. (1984). Play in hospital settings. In T. Yawkey & A. Pellegrini (Eds.), *Play: Developmental and applied.* Hillsdale, NJ: Earlbaum.

Bolig, R. (1988). Guest editorial: The diversity and complexity of play in health care settings. *Children's Health Care, 16* (3), 132-133.

Bolig, R. (1990). Play in health care settings: A challenge for the 1990's. *Children's Health Care, 19* (4), 229-233.

Bolig, R., Fernie, D.E., & Klein, E.L. (1986). Unstructured play in hospital settings: An internal locus of control rationale. *Children's Health Care, 15* (2), 101-107.

Bolig, R. & Weddle, K.D. (1988). Resiliency and hospitalization of children. *Children's Health Care, 16* (4), 255-260.

Brill, N., Cohen, S., Fauvre, M., Klein, N., Clark, S., & Garcia, L. (1987). Caring for chronically ill children: An innovative approach for care. *Children's Health Care, 16* (2), 105-113.

Burke, S.O. (1986). Risk and competence: A model and studies with handicapped children. *Canadian Journal of Public Health, 77* (1), 40-45.

Carson, D.K., Jenkins, J., & Stout, C.B. (1985). Assessing child life programs: Study model with a small number of subjects. *Children's Health Care, 14* (2), 123-125.

Cataldo, M., Bessman, C., Parker, L., Pearson, J., & Rogers, M. (1979). Behavioral assessment for pediatric intensive care units. *Journal of Applied Behavior Analysis, 12,* 83-97.

Clatworthy, S. (1981). Therapeutic play: effects on hospitalized children. *Children's Health Care, 9* (4), 108-113.

da Silva, G.C. (1984). Awareness of Hispanic cultural issues in the health care setting. *Children's Health Care, 13* (1), 4-10.

DelPo, E.G. & Frick, S.B. (1988). Directed and nondirected play as therapeutic modalities. *Children's Health Care, 16* (4), 261-267.

Douglas, J.W. (1975). Early hospital admissions and later disturbances of behavior and learning. *Developmental Medicine and Child Neurology, 17,* 456-480.

Dunst, C.J., Trivette, C.M., Davis, M., & Weeldreyer, J.C. (1988). Enabling and empowering families of children with health impairments. *Children's Health Care, 17* (2), 71-81.

Erikson, E. (1950). *Childhood and society.* New York: Norton.

Featherstone, H. (1981). *A difference in the family: Living with a disabled child.* Harmondsworth, Middlesex, England: Penguin.

Freud, S. (1955). Beyond the pleasure principle. In *Complete psychological works of Sigmund Freud, 18.* London: Hogarth Press.

Gaynard, L., Wolfer, J., Goldberger, J., Thompson, R., Redburn, L., & Laidley, L. (1990). *Psychosocial care of children in hospitals: A clinical practice manual from the ACCH Child Life Research Project.* Washington, D.C.: ACCH.

Gibbons, M.B. & Boren, H. (1985). Stress reduction. *Nursing Clinics of North America, 20* (1), 83-103.

Green, E.C. (1983). Normalization: Meeting growth and development needs of children in pediatric intensive care unit. *Children's Health Care, 12* (1), 43-44.

Johnson, B.H. (1990). The changing role of families in health care. *Children's Health Care, 19* (4), 234-241.

Magrab, P.R. (1985). Psychosocial development of chronically ill children. In N. Hobbs & J.M. Perrin (Eds.), *Issues in the care of children with chronic illness* (pp. 698-716). San Francisco: Jossey-Bass Inc.

Manio, E.B. & Hall, R.R. (1987). Asian family traditions and their influence in transcultural health care delivery. *Children's Health Care, 15* (3), 172-177.

McLane, J.B. (1986). Lekotek: A unique play library for families with handicapped children. *Children's Health Care, 14* (3), 178-182.

Niederhauser, V.P. (1989). Health care of immigrant children: Incorporating culture into practice. *Pediatric Nursing, 15* (6), 569-574.

Oremland, E.K. (1988). Mastering developmental and critical experiences through play and other expressive behaviors in childhood. *Children's Health Care, 16* (3), 150-156.

Pearson, J., Cataldo, M., Tureman, A.,

Bessman, C. & Rogers, M. (1980). Pediatric intensive care unit patients: Effects of play intervention on behavior. *Critical Care Medicine, 8,* 64-67.

Perrin, E.C. & Gerrity, P.S. (1984). Development of children with chronic illness. *Pediatric Clinics of North America, 31,* 19-31.

Petrillo, M. & Sanger, S. (1981). *Emotional care of hospitalized children.* Philadelphia: J.B. Lippincott Co.

Piaget, J. (1962). *Play, dreams and imitation in childhood.* Philadelphia: J.B. Lippincott Co.

Pilon, B.H. & Smith, K.A. (1985). A parent group for the Hispanic parents of children with severe cerebral palsy. *Children's Health Care, 14* (2), 96-102.

Powell, G.J. (Ed.). (1983). *The psychosocial development of minority children.* New York: Brunner/Mazel Inc.

Prugh, D., Staub, E., Sands, H., Kirschbaum, R., & Lenihan, E. (1953). A study of the emotional reactions of children and families to hospitalization and illness. *American Journal of Orthopsychiatry, 23,* 70-106.

Quinton, D. & Rutter, M. (1976). Early hospital admissions and later disturbances of behavior: An attempted replication of Douglas' findings. *Developmental Medicine and Child Neurology, 18,* 447-459.

Ritter, F.L. & Klinzing, M. B. (1980). FPO-For Parents Only. *Children's Health Care, 9* (2), 31-34.

Schaefer, C. (Ed.). (1976). *The therapeutic use of child's play.* New York: Aronson.

Skipper, J.K. & Leonard, R.C. (1968). Children, stress, and hospitalization: A field experiment. *Journal of Health and Social Behavior, 9,* 275-287.

Sponseller, D. (Ed.). (1974). *Play as a learning medium.* Washington, D.C.: National Association for the Education of Young Children.

Thompson, R.H. (1985). *Psychosocial research on pediatric hospitalization and health care: A review of the literature.* Springfield, Il: Charles C. Thomas.

Thompson, R.H., & Stanford, G. (1981). *Child life in hospitals.* Springfield, Il: Charles C. Thomas, Publisher.

van Breda, A. (1989). Health issues facing Native American children. *Pediatric Nursing, 15* (6), 575-577.

Vernon, D., Foley, J., Sipowicz, R., & Schulman, J. (1965). *The psychological responses of children to hospitalization and illness.* Springfield, Il: Charles C. Thomas, Publisher.

West, B.E. (1983). The new arrivals from Southeast Asia. *Childhood Education, 60(2),* 84-89.

Williams, Y.B. & Powell, M. (1980). Documenting the value of supervised play in a pediatric ambulatory care clinic. *Journal of the Association for the Care of Children's Health, 9,* 15-20.

Willis, D.J., Elliott, C.H., & Jay, S.M. (1982). Psychological effects of physical illness and its concomitants. In J.M. Tuma (Ed.), *Handbook for the practice of pediatric psychology.* (pp. 28-66). New York: Wiley.

Wilson, B., Hausslein, E., & McCormick, D. (1982). The pediatric office: New directions for the care of families. *Children's Health Care: Journal of the Association for the Care of Children's Health, 11,* 82-83.

Wilson, J.M. (1988). Future of play in health care settings. *Children's Health Care, 16* (3), 231-237.

Winnicott, D.W. (1965). *The maturational processes and the facilitating environment.* New York: International Universities Press.

Wolfer, J., Gaynard, L., Goldberger, J., Laidley, L., & Thompson, R. (1988). An experimental evaluation of a model child life program. *Children's Health Care, 16* (4), 244-254.

CHAPTER

2

ADMISSION ACTIVITIES

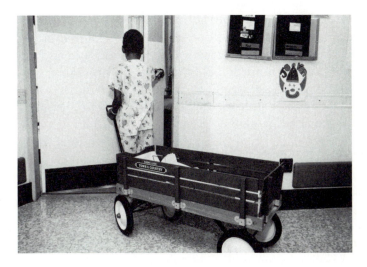

Fig. 2-1 Welcome wagon.

A child's admission into the hospital has been identified as a critical period, or stress point, when interventions are needed to help the child deal effectively with the experience (O'Donnell, 1976: Savedra & Tesler, 1981; Wolfer & Visintainer, 1975; Youssef, 1981). The activities in this chapter offer a variety of ways to address the issues related to a child's admission stress. These types of interventions should be implemented when the child is admitted to the unit and used periodically in ongoing attempts to promote coping and adaptation. Ideally, parents and educators have already performed preadmission activities so that hospital activities will follow up and confirm what the child has already learned (Arzarnoff, 1983; Mather, 1988; Thompson & Stanford, 1981). Admissions activities are even more important when no preadmission preparation has occurred, as in emergency admissions.

BACKGROUND INFORMATION

Children can exhibit a wide range of reactions to hospitalization, but these reactions can be grouped into three types: overt or active responses, passive responses, and regressive responses (Thompson & Stanford, 1981). Some children react to hospitalization with overt, or active, responses such as crying, resisting treatment, or being destructive to the environment, while others exhibit passive responses such as excessive sleeping, decreased eating, or decreased communication and activity. A third group may regress developmentally to behaviors typical of a younger child, such as throwing temper tantrums, exhibiting toileting problems, or becoming more dependent on parents. A child's reactions depend on such variables as his prehospital personality, his social class and ethnic background, the amount of preparation he has had, and his previous hospital experiences. These reactions are indications of the need for admission activities. Parents or other significant others should be consulted regarding the reactions of children so that the professional has a better understanding of each child's response before, during, and after admissions activities.

Health care professionals should also understand the special concerns of various age groups (Thompson & Stanford, 1981). For example, separation from parents or significant others is a great concern for infants, toddlers, and preschool-

ers. Providing concrete information helps prevent magical thinking and misconceptions in preschoolers, while also being helpful to most school-age and adolescent patients. Involvement with peers is important for these older groups, too. Admission activities appropriate for the developmental stage and concerns of pediatric patients should be selected. Adaptations for special needs children may need to be made.

Other characteristics of the child and family must be considered when selecting and implementing admission activities (see Beuf, 1979). One of these is the family system itself since more children are now living in nontraditional homes. Ethnic and social class factors may influence the presence and involvement of extended family members, as well as the communication styles of these people. Bilingual children or those from other cultures may respond differently to interventions. It is important to remember all of these variables when planning and conducting admission activities.

SPECIAL CONSIDERATIONS

Admissions activities assist the health care professional to contact and establish rapport with a child and family in a supportive and nonthreatening way. The activities can promote a smooth transition into the health care system. For those children who were prepared before their admission, the activities will reinforce what they were told and therefore promote trust.

During the admissions activities children seek information and express concerns in a variety of ways. Health care professionals should be sure to observe both the nonverbal and verbal communications of a child. While engaging in the activities, the professional will be able to discern a variety of factors about a child: age appropriateness of behavior, emotional maturity, handicapping conditions, ability to comprehend directions or information, and acquired skills. Psychological indicators that should be considered during these observations include the number of hospital admissions, family support system, stress factors in the home at the time of admission, and reason for admission. These observations can help the professional select additional activities found in this and other chapters.

An important component of these admission

activities is the opportunity they provide for the health care professional to address the needs of the child and family. Information from the activities can be shared with other professionals when appropriate. Ancillary professionals can be brought into the treatment process when warranted. Most importantly, the activities provide the health care professional with information to develop an individualized intervention program for a child and produce the ways and means for follow-up.

ACTIVITY GOALS

The activities in this chapter can be grouped into four major intervention strategies: providing information, encouraging normalization, using familial and other support systems, and identifying coping techniques.

Providing Information

The coping behavior most often used by children who are confronted with a new health care experience is *orienting,* e.g., attempts to learn about the new environment (Hyson, 1983; Savedra & Tesler, 1981; Youssef, 1981). Orienting behaviors can help the child reduce the physical unfamiliarity of the hospital as well as the procedural unfamiliarity of what happens there. Activities that support the orienting responses of children include "Hospital Story," "Look Who Landed in our Hospital," "Scavenger Hunt," "Welcome Wagon Committee," and "Unit Tour." These activities enable children to learn information about their surroundings. Gaining this knowledge is an important way that children can attempt to gain control over the stressful situation.

Encouraging Normalization

Another aspect that makes admission to the hospital stressful is that normal routines are disrupted in an unfamiliar environment. Attempts to make the hospital environment more similar to home are part of the process called *normalization.*

Activities that promote normalization include "Art Cart," "Door Sign," "Privacy Signs," and "What Do You Like to Do?" Through these activities the child can identify his or her own space and have control over it. The child is recognized as a unique person with likes and dislikes.

Using Familial and Other Support Systems

Hospitalized children usually express concern over family separation and view the presence of parents as important for minimizing discomfort (Astin, 1977; Tesler et al, 1981). Activities that promote discussion of the family (or other support network if a traditional family is not present) can help reinforce the important emotional connection between the child and significant others as well as give the health care professional an understanding of familial issues that may need to be addressed. The "All About Me," "Family Tree," and "Special People Bank" activities can accomplish this. Familial involvement with the child can also be encouraged through "Parent Tapes."

Some of the previously listed activities that involve interactions among patients can encourage supportive relationships between patients. These relationships can be particularly helpful for adolescents (Thompson & Stanford, 1981).

Identifying Coping Techniques

Hospitalized children have greater difficulty than healthy children in identifying coping techniques that they can use to deal with a hospital experience (Tesler et al, 1981). Health care professionals can help children recognize coping strategies and understand their meanings. Activities like "Imaginary Vacation," "The Key To Making the Best of a Bad Situation," and "Steps to a Quick Recovery" encourage discussion of coping techniques. They also indicate to the child that he or she will be discharged from the hospital, an underlying concern of many children.

A C T I V I T Y 2 - 1	*ALL ABOUT ME*

Age Group	5 through 10 years
Patient/Staff Ratio	1:1
Approximate Length	15 minutes
Therapeutic Rationale	To promote familial and other support systems by: • Identifying important people and important characteristics of the child
Precautions and Restrictions	Children may need assistance filling in information on the worksheet. Check marker precautions.
Required Skills	Coloring Writing
Equipment	"All About Me" worksheet (Figs. 2-2 and 2-3) Crayons or markers Pencils
Implementation	1. Help the child fill in the sheet and decorate it using crayons or markers. 2. After checking hospital policies regarding the hanging of wall items, with the child's permission, hang the sheet in the patient's room.

ALL ABOUT ME

1 My name is _____

2 I am _____ years old. 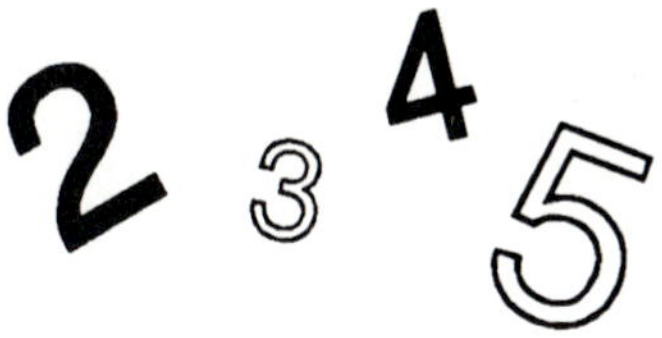 **2** 3 **4** 5

3 The people I live with are:

4 My favorite foods are:

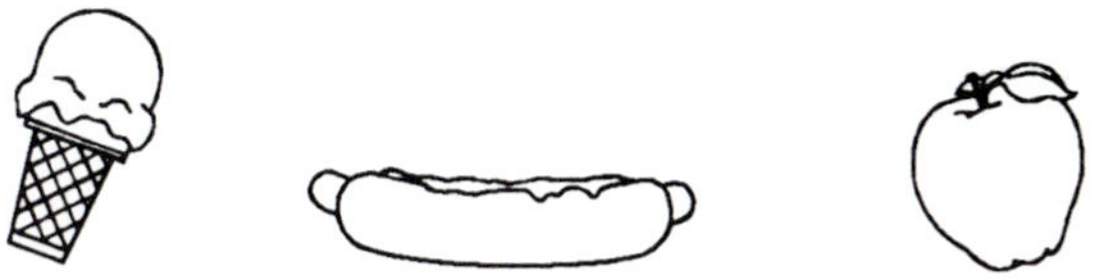

5 What I do best is:

6 My favorite games are:

7 Things that make me happy are:

8 Things that I do not like are:

9 I am here because:

Fig. 2-2

ALL ABOUT ME

1   My name is _____

2   My school is _____
and I'm in the _____ grade.

3   I live at_____
and the people who live with me are:

4   The things I like to do are:

5   The thing I do best is:

6   My favorite subject at school is:

7   My favorite teacher is _____ 
because:

8   My favorite TV program is:

9   The things I don't like are:

10   This is my _____ time in the hospital and I came here
because:

Fig. 2-3

A C T I V I T Y 2 - 2	*ART CART*

Age Group	10 years through adolescence
Patient/Staff Ratio	1:1
Approximate Length	10 minutes
Therapeutic Rationale	To provide normalization by: • Allowing the child to identify and to have an impact on his or her space.
Precautions and Restrictions	Certain institutions may have policies regarding the hanging of items on the wall. Obtain necessary administrative approval before initiating this activity.
Required Skills	None
Equipment	Collection of inexpensive art prints and posters that would appeal to adolescents and school-age children. Pictures should be dry mounted and ready for hanging. Video and record stores may be a good source of donations. Cart Materials to hang pictures (nails, hammer, Velcro, or other technique of choice).
Implementation	1. Have permanently placed picture hangers mounted in each room on the unit. 2. Place the posters on a designated cart. 3. Allow the child to select prints or posters that are appealing and hang them in his or her room.

ACTIVITY 2-3	*DOOR SIGN*

Age Group	5 years through adolescence
Patient/Staff Ratio	5:1
Approximate Length	30 minutes
Therapeutic Rationale	To encourage normalization by: • Allowing the child to identify personal space • Providing feelings of control • Supporting the child's uniqueness and individuality
Precautions and Restrictions	Children without the use of both hands will need assistance. Check glitter, glue, scissor, and marker precautions. The iron should only be used under strict supervision.
Required Skills	Writing or printing Cutting Pasting
Equipment	Posterboard Markers Crayons Paint Glitter Waxed paper Crayon shavings Scissors Chalk Iron Glue or paste

Implementation	1. Discuss the reasons for making a door sign with the child (personally identifies the hospital room and serves as an introduction to other children on the unit).
	2. Give the child a choice of materials and make suggestions about how to design the door sign.
	3. Suggestions for door signs include:
	   a. Writing his or her name in an artistic motif on the poster board with chalk, crayon, or marker.
	   b. Writing his or her name on the poster board with glue and sprinkling glitter over it.
	   c. Ironing crayon shavings between two pieces of waxed paper, cutting out decorative waxed paper letters, and gluing them to the poster board.
	4. With the child's permission, display the sign on the door of the room.

A C T I V I T Y 2 - 4	*FAMILY TREE*

Age Group	5 through 12 years
Patient/Staff Ratio	1:1
Approximate Length	45 minutes
Therapeutic Rationale	To identify potential familial and other support systems by: • Identifying the child's family structure • Determining members of the family living with the child • Facilitating discussion about the family
Precautions and Restrictions	Do not assume a child has a traditional family unit. Some children may hesitate to reveal information about the family. Do not push reluctant children. Check glue, scissor, and marker precautions.
Required Skills	Tracing Writing or printing Pasting Drawing Cutting Scissors
Equipment	Large piece of colored construction paper or posterboard Colored construction paper (various colors) Cardboard leaf patterns Pencil Glue Marker
Implementation	1. Check the chart for family history. 2. Explain the activity to the child. 3. Instruct the child to draw a large tree trunk and cut it out. Younger children may need assistance. 4. Have the child paste the tree trunk to the large piece of construction paper. 5. Ask the child how many people live at home. Instruct the child to select a leaf pattern and trace enough leaves for everyone in the home. Seasonal colors of construction paper may be used. 6. Have the child cut out leaves and attach them to the tree and a large piece of construction paper (Fig. 2-4). 7. Ask the child to draw a portrait of each family member. Discuss personality traits and relationship with the patient. 8. Cut out portraits and glue them to the leaves. 9. Using the marker, write each family member's name below their picture. 10. With the child's permission, display the picture.
Variations	For spring pictures, substitute apple blossoms or flowers for leaves. For Christmas pictures, substitute a Christmas tree for the tree trunk and Christmas tree ornaments for the leaves. School pictures or family snapshots may be substituted for hand-drawn portraits.

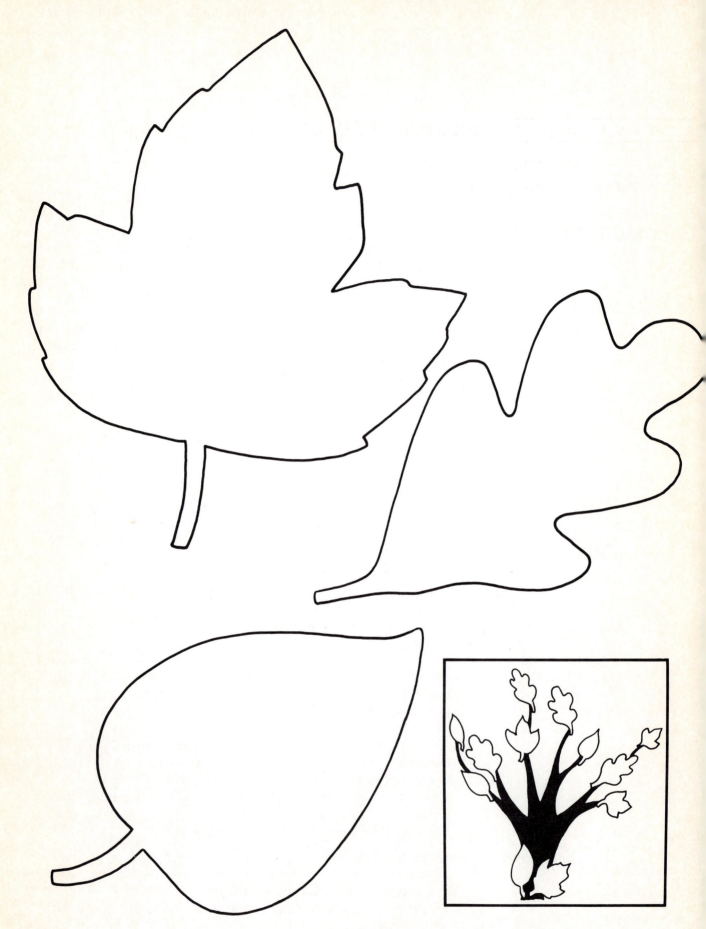

Fig. 2-4

ACTIVITY 2-5	*HOSPITAL STORY*

Age Group	4 through 12 years
Patient/Staff Ratio	5:1 (school-age children) 1:1 (preschool child)
Approximate Length	30 minutes
Therapeutic Rationale	To help provide information about the hospital to the child by: • Orienting the child to the hospital schedule and routines • Identifying specific health care providers on the pediatric unit • Answering questions the child may have about the hospital
Precautions and Restrictions	Children with short attention spans, physical discomfort, or children taking medication that could alter concentration abilities will need two sessions to complete the activity. Some children may need a 1:1 session, contingent on their diagnosis.
Required Skills	Coloring
Equipment	Hospital storybook, preferably large with colorful pictures Drawing and writing paper (one sheet each) Crayons Pencils
Implementation	1. Read the storybook to younger children, having them identify familiar pictures; or have older children read the story aloud. 2. Ask the children to write or dictate their own stories about coming to the hospital. 3. Encourage the children to illustrate their stories.

ACTIVITY 2-6	*IMAGINARY VACATION*

Age Group 4 through 7 years

Patient/Staff Ratio 1:1

Approximate Length 30 minutes

Therapeutic Rationale To identify coping techniques by:
- Helping the child identify soothing images
- Helping the child practice using imagery so that it can be used in stressful situations later

Precautions and Restrictions Do not divert the children from healthy expressions of feelings.

Required Skills None

Equipment Collection of pictures that can be used to design an imaginary vacation.

Implementation
1. Allow the child to look at the pictures and select the places he or she would like to visit.
2. Make a game out of taking an imaginary trip to the places the child selected, discussing what you would see and feel.
3. If necessary, later during the hospital admission, play the game again in situations such as painful procedures and acute episodes of home sickness and separation anxiety.

A C T I V I T Y 2 - 7	*THE KEY TO MAKING THE BEST OF A BAD SITUATION*

Age Group 7 through 12 years

Patient/Staff Ratio 5:1

Approximate Length 30 minutes

Therapeutic Rationale To identify and encourage coping techniques by:
- Discussing the tolerable aspects of the hospital
- Creating a reminder of these aspects that a child may have in his or her room

Precautions and Restrictions Children without the use of both hands will need assistance.
Check marker precautions.

Required Skills Writing
Coloring

Equipment "THE KEY" worksheets (Fig. 2-5)
Pencil or pen (for each participant)
Markers
Crayons

Implementation
1. Provide each child with a "KEY" worksheet.
2. Facilitate a discussion about the hospital emphasizing the positive aspects (e.g., meeting new people, having one's own television, playroom), coping strategies (e.g., maintaining a positive attitude).
3. Have the child write each aspect identified as positive on the "KEY" worksheet.
4. Allow the child to color or decorate the "KEY" as desired.
5. Encourage the child to hang the "KEY" at bedside.

The Key

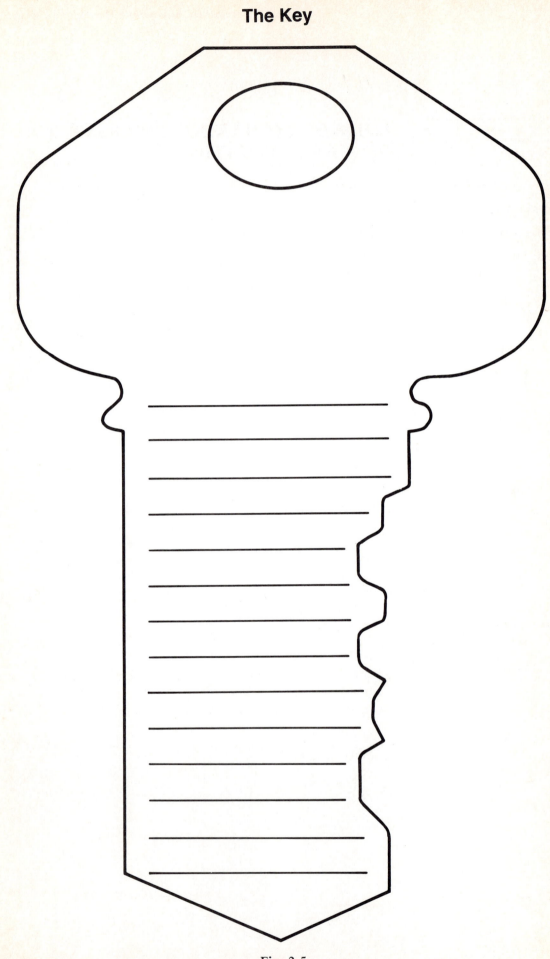

The Key

Fig. 2-5

A C T I V I T Y 2 - 8	*LOOK WHO LANDED IN OUR HOSPITAL*

Age Group
5 through 12 years

Patient/Staff Ratio
6:1

Approximate Length
10 minutes

Therapeutic Rationale
To promote support systems by:
- Introducing children recently admitted to the hospital to other patients
- Increasing socialization among new and old patients

Precautions and Restrictions
Children without the use of both hands will need assistance.
Signed photo consents must be obtained from the family before photographing a child.
Children on bedrest and isolation will not be able to see the bulletin board. An instant photograph of the bulletin board may be taken to show the child.
Check glue and scissor precautions.

Required Skills
Gluing or pasting
Writing

Equipment
Instant camera
Film
Scissors
Bulletin board
Construction paper
Glue
Stapler
Thumbtacks

Implementation
1. Design a spaceship bulletin board. Windows in the ship can represent hospital rooms and beds. Hang the bulletin board in the playroom or hallway.
2. Using the instant camera, take a picture of each child on admission to the hospital.
3. Instruct the child to glue the picture to a piece of construction paper.
4. Have the child write his or her name on the construction paper underneath the picture.
5. Hang each child's picture on the bulletin board.
6. Discuss the names and room numbers of other children with the newly admitted child.

A C T I V I T Y 2 - 9	*PARENT TAPES*

Age Group	Infants through 7 years
Patient/Staff Ratio	1:1
Approximate Length	15 minutes
Therapeutic Rationale	To use the support systems available to the child by: • Having the parents/significant others make an audiotape that can be played during their absence • Decreasing separation anxiety for the child and family
Precautions and Restrictions	Parents should understand the tapes cannot be substituted for a visit. Parents must be willing to make the tapes. The child's response to the tapes must be assessed.
Required Skills	Listening
Equipment	Tape recorder Tape
Implementation	1. Tape parents' messages, the parents reading a story, or conversations between the child and the parents. 2. Play the recording to the child during the parents' absence.
Variation	Have parents create videotapes of special events that happen at home or school during the child's hospitalization.

A C T I V I T Y 2 - 1 0	*PRIVACY SIGNS*

Age Group	9 years through adolescence
Patient/Staff Ratio	5:1
Approximate Length	20 minutes
Therapeutic Rationale	To encourage normalization by: • Identifying personal space • Acknowledging the child's need for privacy • Supporting the child's uniqueness and individuality
Precautions and Restrictions	Participants must have the use of one hand. Check glue and glitter precautions.
Required Skills	Writing Coloring
Equipment	Posterboard Pencil Glitter Eraser Newspaper Glue
Implementation	1. Facilitate a discussion about the needs and rights to privacy. 2. Distribute pencils, erasers, and posterboard to each patient. 3. Have each child design a privacy sign that best suits his or her needs, such as "Do Not Disturb." 4. Once the sign has been drawn, instruct the patient to fill in one letter with glue. Sprinkle glitter over the glue. Shake excess glitter from the poster and repeat the procedure until the poster is completed. 5. Display the poster on the patient's room door when privacy is desired.

A C T I V I T Y   2 - 1 1   *SCAVENGER HUNT*

Age Group	6 through 12 years
Patient/Staff Ratio	5:1
Approximate Length	30 minutes
Therapeutic Rationale	To help provide information about the hospital by:

- Orienting patients to the pediatric unit
- Familiarizing patients with medical equipment
- Interacting with staff and other patients

Precautions and Restrictions

Patients must understand the rules of the game.
Children should know what areas of the unit are included in the hunt.

Required Skills

Reading

Equipment

Unit map
Paper bag
Adhesive bandages (2)
Piece of blue yarn
Piece of red yarn
Pair of slippers
Tongue depressors (2)
Syringe
Straw
Alcohol swabs (3)
List of objects to be found
List of rules of the game

Implementation

1. Place objects in commons areas of the unit such as the public toilet, kitchen, and play areas.
2. Provide each child a list of rules, items to be found and their location, and a map of the unit.
3. Give each child a small paper bag to carry those objects found.
4. Instruct children to locate as many objects as they can in a specified period of time.

A C T I V I T Y 2 - 1 2	*SPECIAL PEOPLE BANK*

Age Group   4 through 8 years

Patient/Staff Ratio   1:1

Approximate Length   20 to 30 minutes

Therapeutic Rationale   To promote familial and other support systems by:
- Identifying the child's family structure
- Determining members of the family living with the child
- Facilitating discussion about the family

Precautions and Restrictions   None

Required Skills   Ability to play symbolically

Equipment   A collection of dolls representing all ages and races

Implementation
1. Ask the child to select a doll to represent each member of his or her family.
2. Encourage the child to talk about each family member to determine the child's relationship with that person.
3. Allow the child to keep the dolls throughout the hospitalization so they may be used, if necessary, to help work through issues related to family and separation.

Variation   Puppets can be made to represent family members when the doll collection does not adequately represent age, race, or family situation.

A C T I V I T Y 2 - 1 3	*STEPS TO A QUICK RECOVERY*

Age Group	7 through 12 years
Patient/Staff Ratio	5:1
Approximate Length	30 minutes
Therapeutic Rationale	To identify and encourage coping techniques by: • Helping the child recognize aspects of medical treatment in which cooperation will hasten discharge • Promoting cooperation with medical treatment • Creating a visual display of helpful behaviors
Precautions and Restrictions	Children without the use of both hands will need assistance. Check glue, scissor, and marker precautions.
Required Skills	Cutting Pasting Writing
Equipment	"Ladder" worksheet (Fig. 2-6) Construction paper Markers Scissors Paste
Implementation	1. Have each child identify methods of helping himself or herself recover and ultimately return home, such as eating and taking medicine. 2. Discuss with the group why each suggestion is beneficial. 3. Have the children write their suggestions on strips of colored construction paper. 4. To make the ladder rungs, paste each strip of construction paper on the "Ladder" worksheet. 5. Children may color the rest of the sheet with markers if desired and display the ladder in their rooms.

Fig. 2-6

ACTIVITY 2-14	*UNIT TOUR*

Age Group	4 years through adolescence
Patient/Staff Ratio	1:1
Approximate Length	15 minutes
Therapeutic Rationale	To provide information about the hospital by:

- Orienting children and their families to the pediatric unit
- Identifying specific areas of interest such as the playroom, nurses' station, and clocks
- Introducing the child to other children on the unit

Precautions and Restrictions	Check marker precautions.
Required Skills	None
Equipment	Map of the unit Markers
Implementation	

1. Circle or color the child's room on the map.
2. Walk the child and family around the unit, pointing out areas of interest.
3. Assist the child in locating specific areas on the map.

ACTIVITY 2-15	*WELCOME WAGON COMMITTEE*

Age Group	8 years through adolescence
Patient/Staff Ratio	2:1
Approximate Length	20 minutes
Therapeutic Rationale	To help provide information about the hospital to the child by: • Having the child interact with the staff and other patients • Orienting new patients to hospital routines and procedures • Assessing the interests of new patients
Precautions and Restrictions	None
Required Skills	Reading Writing
Equipment	Admission storybook Interest survey Patient newsletter Unit map Calendar
Implementation	1. Choose a patient who would benefit from social interaction. 2. Ask the patient to help you welcome a new patient to the hospital (see Fig. 2-1). 3. Introduce the two patients. Have the "Welcome Wagon" patient present the new patient with the admission storybook, patient newsletter, unit map, interest survey, and calendar and then accompany the new arrival on a unit tour.

A C T I V I T Y 2 - 1 6	*WHAT DO YOU LIKE TO DO?*

Age Group   5 years through adolescence

Patient/Staff Ratio   1:1

Approximate Length   10 minutes

Therapeutic Rationale   To encourage normalization by:
- Identifying the patient's interests to support his or her own uniqueness
- Providing a choice of activities for the patient to gain a sense of control
- Engaging the patient in the activity selection and planning process

Precautions and Restrictions   None

Required Skills   None

Equipment   Interest survey listing available activities and projects on the unit
Pencil

Implementation
1. Explain to the child that you would like to know more about the activities he or she likes to do.
2. Have the child complete an interest survey of those activities and projects available on the unit. Younger children or visually impaired children can be interviewed.
3. Incorporate the child's interests into daily activity plans.

ADDITIONAL IDEAS

- Create child life admission kits for nurses to distribute when child life staff members are unavailable.
- Design a welcome sign for patients newly admitted, and hang it on the door of the room before the patient arrives.
- Have parents complete a questionnaire that identifies feeding, bath, and bedtime rituals for young children.
- Provide adolescents, infants, and toddlers with inexpensive radios for their room.
- Encourage parents to bring family photographs and favorite toys, blankets, pillows, and pajamas from home.

- Post a list of predictable hospital events such as meal times, rest periods, and medical rounds in each room.
- Post parents' and grandparents' home and work phone numbers in each young child's room for easy access during periods of acute separation anxiety. Be sure to determine if this is acceptable to parents and identify particular times when it may not be appropriate to call.
- Place an article of clothing with Mom's scent in an infant's crib.
- Use bubbles to initiate play at a safe distance from a toddler with a high level of stranger anxiety.

REFERENCES

Astin, E.W. (1977). Self-reported fears of hospitalized and non-hospitalized children aged ten to twelve. *Maternal-Child Nursing Journal, 6,* 17-24.

Azarnoff, P. (Ed.). (1983). *Preparation of young healthy children for possible hospitalization: The issues.* Santa Monica, Ca: Pediatric Projects, Inc.

Beuf, A.H. (1979). *Biting off the bracelet: A study of children in hospitals.* Philadelphia: University of PA Press.

Hyson, M.C. (1983). Going to the doctor: A developmental study of stress and coping. *Journal of Child Psychology and Psychiatry, 24,* 247-259.

Mather, P.L. (1988). Educating preschoolers about health care. *Childhood Education, 65* (2), 94-100.

O'Donnell, R.L. (1976). *The psychological effects of childhood hospitalization: Implications for pediatric health care delivery.* (Doctoral dissertation, University of Iowa, 1976.) *Dissertation Abstracts International,* 1978, *38,* 3121-3122-B. (University Microfilms No. 77-28498.)

Savedra, M. & Tesler, M. (1981). Coping strategies of hospitalized school-age children. *Western Journal of Nursing Research, 3,* 371-384.

Tesler, M.D., Wegner, C., Savedra, M., Gibbons, P.T. & Ward, J.A. (1981). Coping strategies of children in pain. *Issues in Comprehensive Pediatric Nursing, 5,* 351-359.

Thompson, R.H. & Stanford, G. (1981). *Child Life in hospitals: Theory and practice.* Springfield, Il: Charles C. Thomas, Publisher.

Wolfer, J.A. & Visintainer, M.A. (1975). Pediatric surgical patients' and parents' stress responses and adjustment. *Nursing Research, 24,* 244-255.

Youssef, M.M. (1981). Self-control behaviors of school-age children who are hospitalized for cardiac diagnostic procedures. *Maternal-Child Nursing Journal, 10,* 219-284.

CHAPTER 3

BODY IMAGE AND AWARENESS ACTIVITIES

Fig. 3-1 Body molds.

*I*llness and hospitalization can have profound effects on how children and adolescents view their bodies, making the task of forming an accurate and positive body image very difficult. Medical treatment implies some internal or external defect requiring evaluation, treatment, and/or correction. The outcome may produce changes in the body, either temporarily or permanently, that require adjustment at many levels—perceptual, emotional, and behavioral. The activities in this chapter are designed to help identify and reduce body image disturbances. Additional activities addressing self-esteem, self-expression, and group interactions are in other chapters to supplement those in this chapter.

BACKGROUND INFORMATION

Body image is a term that has several meanings (Witt, Cermak & Coster, 1990). It is defined as the individual's feelings and attitudes about his or her own body. It also refers to the mental picture one has of his or her body—its existence, position in space, and parts in relation to each other.

A child's knowledge of the world begins with knowledge of his or her body. After children learn the spatial relationships of their own bodies, they can generalize this information to other objects. This process occurs during the sensorimotor stage of cognitive development and enables children to conceive, organize, and perform new motor tasks. Perceptual and social development are also important in this process. Research (MacWhinney, Cermak & Fischer, 1987; Witt, Cermak & Coster, 1990) indicates that the ability to identify body parts develops rapidly between the ages of 1 and 2 years. According to the findings of Witt, Cermak, and Coster (1990), children first learn the names of those body parts that have received a large amount of sensory input: eyes, nose, mouth, and hair. These are also body parts that babies explore tactually within the first 3 days of life (Kravitz, Goldenberg & Neyhus, 1978). These parts, as well as the other body parts learned first, were also ones that adults tended to point out and discuss. Witt, Cermak, and Coster concluded that between 12 and 24 months, children's increased mobility leads to increased tactile, kinesthetic, proprioceptive, vestibular, and visual stimulation resulting in greater body awareness.

A longer attention span and the development of language skills enable the child to label and point to body parts on themselves and dolls by 2 years of age.

A child's feelings and attitudes about his or her body continue to develop during childhood from personal physical experiences and social interactions (Broadwell, 1985). Other peoples' reactions to the child's appearance influence the way the child sees his body. The child's mastery in several domains, including cognitive, social, and athletic proficiency, support the development of a good body image. The child's perception of his or her body image can affect self-concept and self-esteem. All three concepts are interrelated.

An important component of adolescent development involves developing positive feelings of comfort about body appearance and function (Nelson, 1987; Rutledge & Dick, 1983). This age period can be particularly difficult for the adolescent whose appearance differs significantly from the norm. The tasks of adolescence are carried forward into adulthood, and so is the individual's evolving body image.

Persons' perceptions about themselves and their bodies influence mental health (Austin, Champion & Tzeng, 1989; Stein, 1983). Treatment for a variety of conditions and illnesses may influence body image by altering the physical appearance of the patient. Burn, orthopedic, and cancer patients can be especially challenged by changes in their bodies. These alterations in appearance may cause patients of all ages to become insecure. Descriptive research findings with children indicate that age, as well as the experience of living with an illness requiring medical intervention, are important influences on the way children feel about their bodies (Neff, 1990). Low body satisfaction is associated with anxiety and insecurity in early studies with adolescent and adult age groups (Douty, Moore & Hartford, 1974; Lerner & Karabenick, 1974; Lerner, Orlos & Knapp, 1976; Rosen & Ross, 1968, Secord & Jourard, 1953; Zion, 1965). Subsequent research reveals that poor body image is associated with low self-esteem in obese (Mendelson & White, 1982), cleft lip/palate (Starr, 1982), and burn patients (Bernstein, 1985). Research on personality and behavior differences in groups of boys with short stature indicates that short adolescent males are more inhibited in that they are more conforming, obsessive-compulsive, and less aggressive than younger boys with short stature. In the same study both older and younger boys were significantly more withdrawn than peers their age as measured by an objective personality test (Holmes, Hayford & Thompson, 1982). Teri (1982) found body image to be an important predictor of depression in high school students. College-aged bulimic women had lower self-esteem and body image than a control group in research by Katzman and Wolchik (1984). Interventions to improve body image have resulted in increased self-concept with prepubescent girls (Kerrins, 1983) and adult women (Dworkin & Kerr, 1987).

SPECIAL CONSIDERATIONS

The developmental progression of body image development is a consideration when selecting interventions for body image disturbances. Just as the young child learns about body parts and then their functioning, health care professionals can offer sequential therapeutic play activities that promote this knowledge. If the child knows body parts, then activities enabling the child to learn more about body functions can be used. Misconceptions can be remediated during the process. Accepting the body is another experiential level that can then be promoted through therapeutic play activities.

Children and adolescents should always be allowed to choose whether to participate in body image activities since the activity may be threatening to them. When conducting activities in groups, make sure that the group is sensitive to each individual.

ACTIVITY GOALS

The activities in this chapter have several goals: to increase knowledge about external and internal body parts, to increase knowledge about body functions, and to increase acceptance of the body.

Learning About External Body Parts

Learning about external body parts is an important developmental milestone. Activities include "Life-Size Self-Portraits," "Body Awareness for Babies," and "Shadow Dancing."

Learning About Internal Body Parts

Internal body parts are also part of a person's body image, even though they are not visible. Activities to promote knowledge about these body parts include: "Me The Inside Story," "Pin the Organ on the Body," and "X-ray Guessing Game."

Learning About Body Functions

Knowledge of body parts alone is not enough. Knowing how the body functions helps in understanding how to care for it. Activities that encourage this goal include "Body Drawings," "Body Puzzles," and "Coloring Body Parts."

Body Acceptance

As people learn about their bodies and how they work, they also develop an attitude about themselves. Acceptance of one's body is an important goal of activities like "Body Outlines," "Makeup Makeover," "Photo Ornaments," "Body Molds," and "Silhouettes."

A C T I V I T Y   3 - 1

BODY AWARENESS FOR BABIES

Age Group	9 to 36 months
Patient/Staff Ratio	1:1
Approximate Length	5 to 10 minutes
Therapeutic Rationale	To increase knowledge about external body parts by: • Naming facial features on a doll • Locating and identifying facial features of the child and doll
Precautions and Restrictions	None
Required Skills	None
Equipment	Doll Mirror
Implementation	1. Show the child a doll. Allow touching for a few minutes. 2. Begin to identify body parts on the doll, repeating their names frequently. 3. Hold the mirror in front of the child and identify his or her body parts. 4. Continue the activity as long as the child maintains interest.

A C T I V I T Y 3 - 2	*BODY DRAWING*

Age Group   5 through 9 years

Patient/Staff Ratio   5:1

Approximate Length   15 minutes

Therapeutic Rationale   To increase knowledge about how the body functions by:
    • Drawing a body
    • Naming the function of each part drawn

Precautions and Restrictions   Check marker precautions.
Participants must have the use of both hands.

Required Skills   Pasting
Drawing

Equipment   Magazine pictures of various body parts (e.g., nose, foot)
Paste
Markers or pencils (depending on the child's age)
Drawing paper

Implementation
1. Paste a picture of a specific body part on a sheet of drawing paper.
2. Instruct the child to draw a complete person around the picture of the body part.
3. Discuss the picture with the child, emphasizing the names and functions of the various body parts.

A C T I V I T Y   3 - 3   *BODY MOLDS*

Age Group	8 through 12 years
Patient/Staff Ratio	6:1
Approximate Length	30 minutes
Therapeutic Rationale	To increase acceptance of the body by: • Constructing a life-size image of the patient's own body from aluminum foil
Precautions and Restrictions	Check scissor precautions. Participants must have the use of both hands.
Required Skills	Cutting
Equipment	Heavy-duty aluminum foil Tape Scissors Hole puncher String or yarn

Implementation

1. Cut two sheets of foil for each child. The length of the foil should exceed the height of the child by at least 8 inches. Tape the two sheets of foil together lengthwise.
2. Have the child lie down on the floor.
3. The activity leader should then *gently* mold the foil to the child's face and body (Fig. 3-2, *A*).
4. Lift the foil off very carefully, so as not to distort the mold (Fig. 3-2, *B*).
5. Have the child cut away the excess foil.
6. If desired, punch holes in the forms, insert string or yarn, and hang the forms on the walls or from the ceiling (Fig. 3-2, *C*).

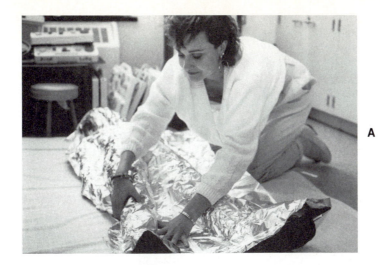

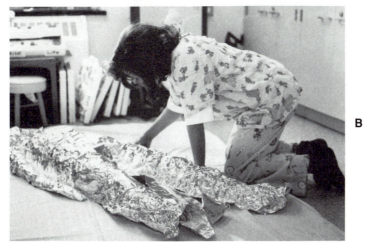

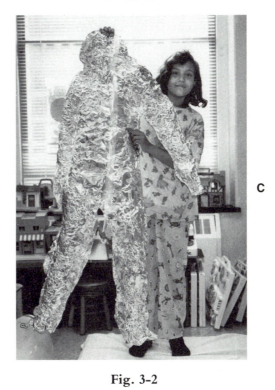

Fig. 3-2

A C T I V I T Y   3 - 4

BODY OUTLINES

Age Group	4 through 12 years
Patient/Staff Ratio	5:1
Approximate Length	30 minutes
Therapeutic Rationale	To increase acceptance of the body by: • Coloring clothes onto a body outline • Drawing facial features onto a body outline • Displaying the body outline in the hospital room
Precautions and Restrictions	Participants must have the use of both hands and be ambulatory. Check marker and scissor precautions.
Required Skills	Cutting
Equipment	Scissors Large roll of newsprint or butcher paper Markers Paint
Implementation	1. Cut a piece of newsprint or butcher paper for each child. The paper should be approximately 8 inches longer than the child is tall. 2. Have the child lie down on the floor on top of the paper. 3. Trace an outline of the child's body. Avoid pressing too closely to the child's body, since it will distort the shape. 4. Instruct the child to cut out the body outline and color or paint features, hair, and clothing. 5. Encourage the child to display the finished product in his or her room.

A C T I V I T Y 3 - 5	*BODY PUZZLES*
Age Group	4 through 7 years
Patient/Staff Ratio	5:1
Approximate Length	30 minutes
Therapeutic Rationale	To increase knowledge about body functions by: • Assembling a body puzzle • Naming and describing the function of the body parts assembled
Precautions and Restrictions	Child must be able to use one hand.
Required Skills	None
Equipment	Cardboard Markers Scissors
Implementation	1. To make the puzzles, draw a body outline on cardboard and cut it out. 2. Cut the body outline into pieces. The number of pieces will be contingent on the age of the child. (Five-to six-piece puzzles work well with children 5 years old.) 3. Give the child the puzzle pieces with instructions to assemble the body. 4. Have the child name the parts of the body and their function as the puzzle is constructed.

A C T I V I T Y 3 - 6	*COLORING BODY PARTS*

Age Group 4 through 7 years

Patient/Staff Ratio 5:1

Approximate Length 15 minutes

Therapeutic Rationale To increase knowledge about body functions by:
- Coloring the appropriate body part, when instructed
- Discussing the function of each part colored

Precautions and Restrictions Participants must have the use of one hand.
Check marker precautions.

Required Skills Coloring
Must know colors

Equipment Body outline
Crayons or markers

Implementation
1. Direct child to color each part on the body outline a specific color (e.g., arms, blue; head, green; legs, yellow).
2. As each part is colored, ask about the function of that particular part.
3. Have the child point to the part on his or her own body.

Variation This activity may be used as part of pretreatment teaching, having the child color in the area where surgery or treatment will occur.

ACTIVITY 3-7	*LIFE-SIZE SELF-PORTRAITS*

Age Group 7 through 12 years

Patient/Staff Ratio 5:1

Approximate Length 30 minutes

Therapeutic Rationale To increase knowledge about external body parts by:
- Drawing a full-length, life-size self-portrait
- Discussing own unique physical characteristics

Precautions and Restrictions The participants must have the use of both hands and be ambulatory. Check marker precautions.

Required Skills Coloring
Drawing

Equipment Pencil
Markers
Butcher paper or examining table paper
Tape
Full-length mirror

Implementation
1. Tape sheets of paper on the wall, extending from the floor to a height several inches taller than the child.
2. Let the children take turns studying themselves in the full-length mirror. Discuss each child's physical attributes. Point out the proportional size of his or her legs and arms to the size of the torso. Emphasize unique physical characteristics, such as large blue eyes, short blond hair, freckles.
3. Have the child stand with his or her back against the paper. Use the pencil to mark the top of his or her head on the paper.
4. Have the child use markers to create a life-size self-portrait, extending from the floor to the mark on the paper. Allow the child to go back and study himself or herself in the mirror as often as necessary to complete the activity.
5. Encourage the child to include as much detail as possible.

A C T I V I T Y 3 - 8	*MAKEUP MAKEOVER*

Age Group   Adolescence

Patient/Staff Ratio   3:1

Approximate Length   30 minutes

Therapeutic Rationale   To increase acceptance of the body by:
      • Applying makeup to enhance facial features

Precautions and Restrictions   Children should not share cosmetics or applicators that come in direct contact with the skin.
Be sensitive to parental wishes regarding makeup.
Check all participants for history of allergies or any evidence of skin irritation in area where cosmetics will be applied.

Required Skills   None

Equipment   Washcloth
Assorted cosmetics
Stage makeup
Cottonballs
Mild soap
Soap
Acrylic mirrors
Makeup applicators
Water-filled basins
Towels

Implementation   1. Provide each patient with washcloth, towel, basin filled with water, cottonballs, makeup applicators, and soap.
2. Have the participants wash and dry their faces.
3. Encourage the participants to study their reflection in the mirror and apply makeup as desired.

| **A C T I V I T Y   3 - 9** | *ME—THE INSIDE STORY* |

Age Group	7 years through adolescence
Patient/Staff Ratio	5:1
Approximate Length	30 minutes
Therapeutic Rationale	To increase knowledge about internal body parts by: • Naming internal body parts • Drawing each body part named
Precautions and Restrictions	Children must have the use of one hand. Check marker precautions.
Required Skills	Coloring
Equipment	Body outlines of front and back views of child figures Pencil Crayons or markers
Implementation	1. Ask the children to list as many internal organs as they can. 2. Have them draw the internal organs identified on the body outline. 3. Ask the children to describe the function of each body part named. Label the parts accordingly. 4. If the child's drawing or explanations reveal misconceptions, accurate information geared to the child's level of understanding should be provided. 5. When the children have identified all the body parts they can think of, have them color their completed outlines.
Variation	This activity can be limited to specific organs or systems as part of the child's pretreatment teaching. The activity may also be used to evaluate the child's understanding of prior educational activities.

A C T I V I T Y 3 - 1 0	*PHOTO ORNAMENTS*

Age Group 7 through 12 years

Patient/Staff Ratio 5:1

Approximate Length 30 minutes

Therapeutic Rationale To increase acceptance of the body by:
- Constructing a Christmas tree ornament from the patient's photograph

Precautions and Restrictions This activity requires the use of both hands, and photo consents must be obtained.
Check glue and scissor precautions.

Required Skills Cutting
Pasting

Equipment Small photo of the child
Decorative fringe
Glue
Scissors
Waxed paper
Cardboard
Paper clip

Implementation
1. Instruct the children to cut a piece of cardboard the same size as the photograph, and have them glue the cardboard to the back of the photograph.
2. Saturate the decorative fringe in glue.
3. Place the fringe on a sheet of waxed paper forming it into the desired frame shape.
4. Allow the frame to dry, and glue on the photograph.
5. Bend the paper clip to form a hanger for the ornament (Fig. 3-3).

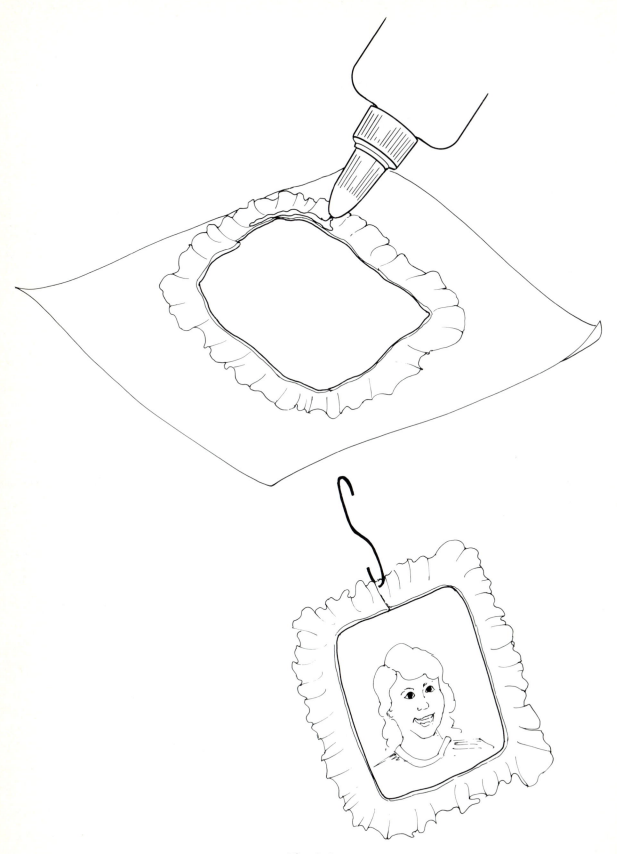

Fig. 3-3

A C T I V I T Y   3 - 1 1

PIN THE ORGAN ON THE BODY

Age Group	8 through 12 years
Patient/Staff Ratio	5:1
Approximate Length	45 minutes
Therapeutic Rationale	To increase knowledge about internal body parts by: • Viewing a body outline with internal organs • Placing cutouts of internal organs in the appropriate places on a body outline
Precautions and Restrictions	This activity requires the use of both hands.
Required Skills	Memorization
Equipment	Tape Cardboard Posterboard, 5′ by 3′ Clear contact paper Markers Organ diagrams (Fig. 3-4, Parts 2, 3, 4, 5, and 6) Scissors Rubber cement
Implementation	1. To make the game, draw a body outline approximately 4 feet high on both sides of the posterboard (Fig. 3-4, Part 1). 2. Color and cut out two sets of organ diagrams. 3. Using rubber cement, attach one set of organs to one body outline. Mount the remaining set of organs on cardboard and cut them out. 4. Cover the body outlines and organs with clear contact paper or have them laminated. 5. Allow the children to view the body outline with the organs for several minutes. 6. Turn the poster around, so they are viewing the blank outline. 7. Give a child the set of organs, and ask him or her to place them in the correct position on the blank outline. Use tape to secure the organs to the outline. 8. Count the number of organs placed correctly on the outline and repeat the activity for each participant. 9. Award participation prizes.

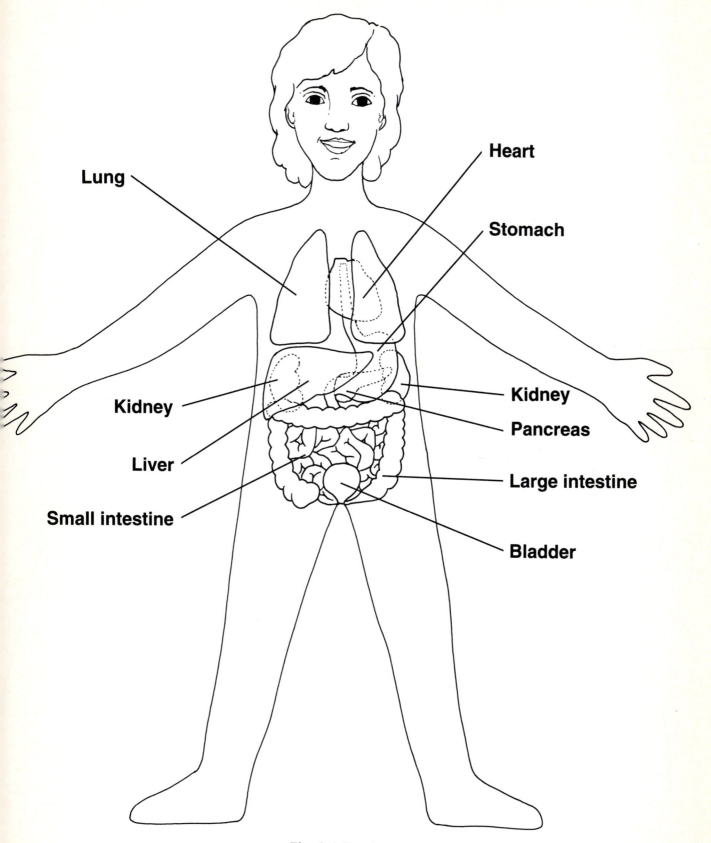

Fig. 3-4 Part 1.

Lungs

The lungs collect oxygen from the air you breathe. The lungs give the oxygen to the blood. The blood gives carbon dioxide to the lungs. The carbon dioxide is exhaled from the body.

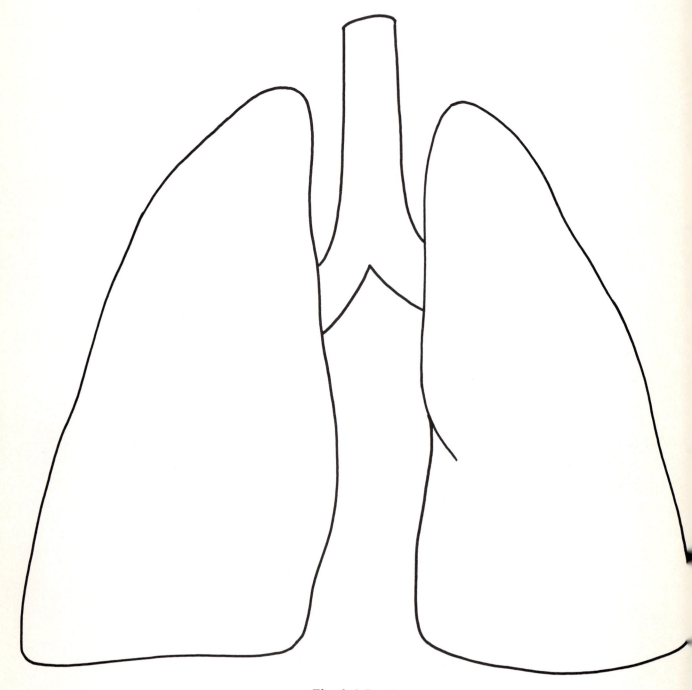

Fig. 3-4 Part 2.

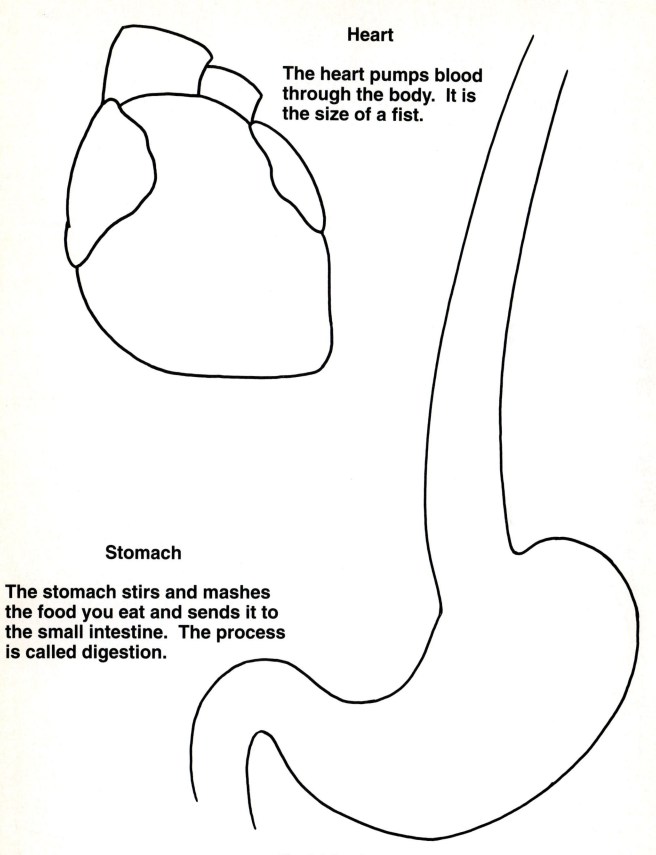

Heart

The heart pumps blood through the body. It is the size of a fist.

Stomach

The stomach stirs and mashes the food you eat and sends it to the small intestine. The process is called digestion.

Fig. 3-4 Part 3.

Pancreas

The pancreas makes "juices" that are needed to help with digestion. The pancreas also makes insulin that helps the body convert sugars into energy.

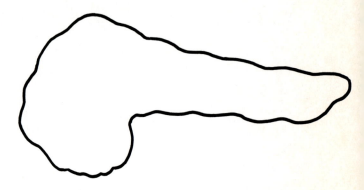

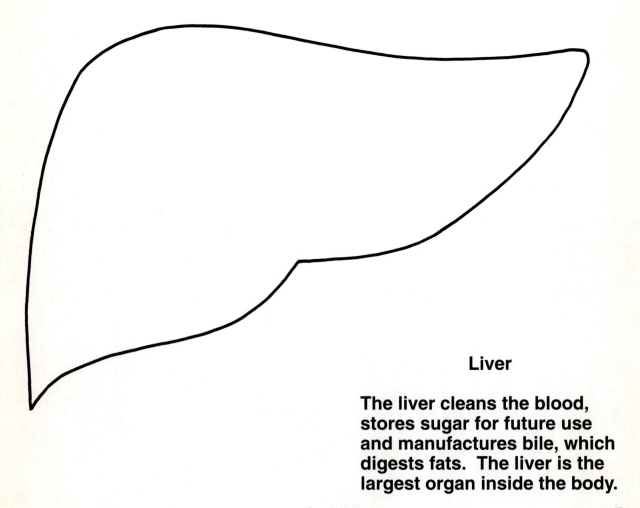

Liver

The liver cleans the blood, stores sugar for future use and manufactures bile, which digests fats. The liver is the largest organ inside the body.

Fig. 3-4 Part 4.

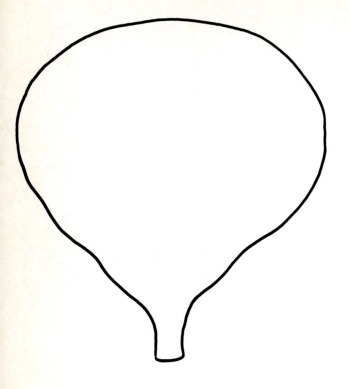

Bladder

The bladder stores urine until it is ready to be released from the body.

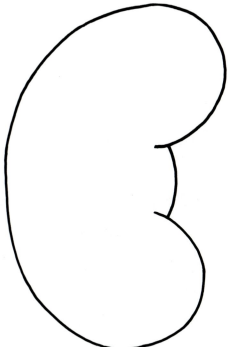

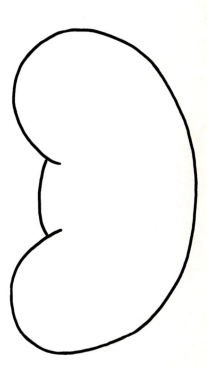

Kidneys

The kidneys clean impurities from the blood. These impurities are combined with water. This is called urine.

Fig. 3-4 Part 5.

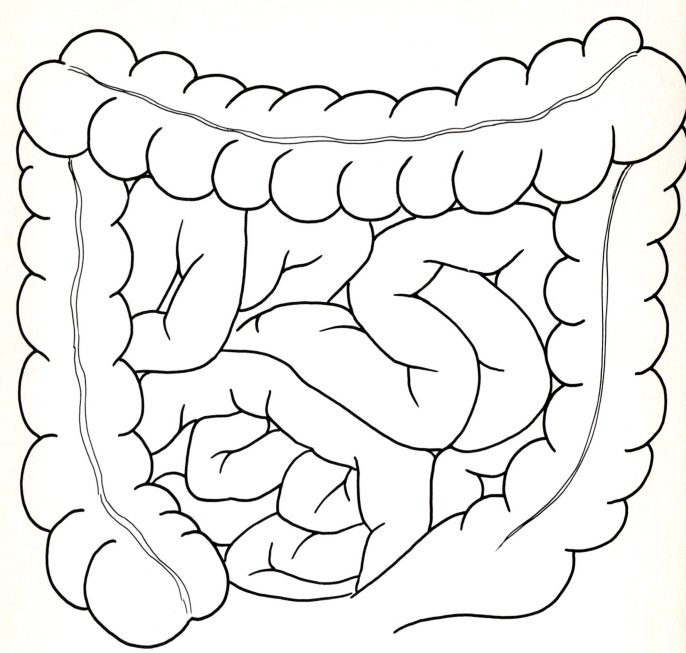

Small Intestines

The small intestines contain ville, which have many tiny blood vessels. The blood absorbs the "food " in the small intestine.

Large Intestines

The large intestines receive the leftover food from the small intestines. The waste leaves the body through the rectum.

Fig. 3-4 Part 6.

A C T I V I T Y 3 - 1 2	*SHADOW DANCING*

Age Group	15 to 36 months
Patient/Staff Ratio	2:1
Approximate Length	15 to 20 minutes
Therapeutic Rationale	To increase awareness of external body parts by: • Moving his or her body to cast different shadows on a sheet or screen
Precautions and Restrictions	Lights in the play area should be dimmed, not shut off.
Required Skills	Walking
Equipment	Slide projector White sheet Tape
Implementation	1. Use the white sheet as a screen. 2. Tape it low enough so the children can touch it. 3. Demonstrate how to shadow dance in the projector light. Encourage the children to participate.

ACTIVITY 3-13   *SILHOUETTES*

Age Group	3 through 12 years
Patient/Staff Ratio	5:2
Approximate Length	30 minutes
Therapeutic Rationale	To increase acceptance of the body by: • Participating in the activity • Completing the project • Displaying the completed project
Precautions and Restrictions	The participants must have the use of one hand. Check glue and scissor precautions.
Required Skills	Cutting Pasting
Equipment	Construction paper Scissors Tape Chair Pencil Lamp or film strip projector Paste or glue
Implementation	1. Have the child sit in a chair placed parallel to the wall. 2. Tape white construction paper to the wall at the same level as the child's head. 3. Position the light source so that it shines directly on the paper. A shadow profile of the child's head will be cast on the paper. 4. Carefully trace the silhouette with a pencil. Be sure to include as much detail as possible (e.g., eyelashes, hair wisps). 5. Have the child carefully cut out the silhouette. 6. Paste the silhouette on a contrasting color of construction paper.

A C T I V I T Y 3 - 1 4	*X-RAY GUESSING GAME*

Age Group 5 through 12 years

Patient/Staff Ratio 5:1

Approximate Length 20 minutes

Therapeutic Rationale To increase knowledge about internal body parts by:
- Identifying body parts depicted on an x-ray film
- Assembling x-ray films to create an image of a body

Precautions and Restrictions This activity requires the use of both hands.
Check scissor precaution.

Required Skills Cutting

Equipment X-ray films★
Light source
Scissors

Implementation
1. Hold an x-ray film to a light source.
2. Have children guess what part of the body is depicted.
3. Have the children point to that part on their own bodies.
4. Ask the children to describe the function of the body part.
5. Continue steps 1 through 4, until all of the x-ray photographs have been discussed.
6. Have the children cut out the x-ray films.
7. When they have been cut out, have the children compile the various pieces to form a completed body.

★X-ray films may be duplicated or copied in the x-ray department.

ADDITIONAL IDEAS

- Play follow the leader or dance to "Hokey Pokey" to encourage movement of specific body parts.
- Videotape the children to promote body image confrontation.
- Keep a selection of inexpensive fashionable hats for chemotherapy patients to use.
- Have a head-scarf–tying class for chemotherapy patients.
- Have commercial body puzzles on hand.

- Place Plexiglass mirrors in the infant's crib to encourage self-discovery.
- Keep an assortment of nail polish and grooming equipment (such as blow dryers and curling irons) for adolescent girls to use.
- Encourage children to wear their own clothing or pajamas whenever possible.
- Recruit a hair stylist to donate time to style older children's hair (get parental permission first).

REFERENCES

Austin, J.K., Champion, V.L., & Tzeng, O. (1989). Cross-cultural relationships between self-concept and body image in high school-age boys. *Archives of Psychiatric Nursing, 3* (4), 234-240.

Bernstein, N.R. (1985). Marital and sexual adjustment of severely burned patients. *Medical Aspects of Human Sexuality, 19* (20), 211-229.

Broadwell, D.C. (1985). Self-concept. In P. Potter & A. Perry (Eds.), *Fundamentals of Nursing: Concepts, process & practice* (1st ed.). St. Louis: Mosby.

Douty, H.T., Moore, J.B., & Hartford, D. (1974). Body characteristics in relation to life adjustment, body image and attitudes of college females. *Journal of Perceptual and Motor Skills, 39,* 399-452.

Dworkin, S.H. & Kerr, B.A. (1987). Comparison of interventions for women experiencing body image problems. *Journal of Counseling Psychology, 34* (2), 136-140.

Holmes, C.S., Hayford, J.T., & Thompson, R.G. (1982). Personality and behavior differences in groups of boys with short stature. *Children's Health Care, 11* (2), 61-64.

Katzman, M.A. & Wolchik, S.A. (1984). Bulimia and binge eating in college women: A comparison of personality and behavioral characteristics. *Journal of Consulting and Clinical Psychology, 52* (3), 423-428.

Kerrins, K.M. (1983). Comparing the self-image of prepubescent girls before and after four sessions of body awareness. *Journal of School Health, 53* (9), 541-543.

Kravitz, H., Goldenberg, D., & Neyhus, A. (1978). Tactual exploration by normal infants. *Developmental Medicine and Child Neurology, 20,* 720-726.

Lerner, R.M. & Karabenick, S.A. (1974). Physical attractiveness, body attitudes, and self-concept in late adolescence. *Journal of Youth and Adolescence, 3* (4), 307-316.

Lerner, R.M., Orlos, J.B., & Knapp, J.R. (1976). Physical attractiveness, physical effectiveness, and self-concept in late adolescence. *Adolescence, 11* (43), 313-326.

MacWhinney, K., Cermak, S., & Fisher, A. (1987). Body part identification in 1- to 4-year-old children. *American Journal of Occupational Therapy, 41,* 454-459.

Mendelson, B.K. & White, D.R. (1982). Relation between body esteem and self-esteem of obese and normal children. *Perceptual and Motor Skills, 54,* 899-905.

Neff, J.A. (1990). Body knowledge and concerns. *Nursing Times, 86* (20), 67-71.

Nelson, A.L. (1987). Normalization: The key to integrating the spinal cord injured patient into the community. *Spinal Cord Injury Nursing, 4* (1), 3-6.

Rosen, G. & Ross, A. (1968). Relationship of body image to self-concept. *Journal of Consulting and Clinical Psychology, 32,* 100.

Rutledge, D.N., & Dick, G. (1983). Spinal cord injury in adolescence. *Rehabilitation Nursing, 8* (6), 8-21.

Secord, S. & Jourard, S. (1953). The appraisal of body cathexis: Body cathexis and the self. *Journal of Consulting Psychology, 17,* 343-347.

Starr, P. (1982). Physical attractiveness and self-esteem ratings of young adults with cleft lip and/or palate. *Psychological Reports, 50,* 467-470.

Stein, R. (1983). Growing up with a physical difference. *Children's Health Care, 12* (2), 53-61.

Teri, L. (1982). Depression in adolescence: Its relationship to assertions and various aspects of self-image. *Journal of Clinical Child Psychology, 11* (2), 101-106.

Witt, A., Cermak, S., & Coster W. (1990). Body part identification in 1- to 2-year old children. *The American Journal of Occupational Therapy, 44* (2), 147-153.

Zion, L. (1965). Body concept as it relates to self-concept. *The Research Quarterly, 36,* 490-495.

CHAPTER

4

GROUP INTERACTION ACTIVITIES

Fig. 4-1 Collaborative proclamations.

*I*lness can separate children from their friends and normal support systems. Group activities with pediatric patients promote new friendships and decrease feelings of isolation. Through activities that involve group interaction, children and adolescents can gain new insights and coping strategies from interacting with peers who are going through the same or similar experiences. Effective peer interaction is a major developmental task of childhood and adolescence; therefore, opportunities for group activities are an important part of a psychosocial treatment plan for pediatric patients. The activities in this chapter will help in this treatment planning.

BACKGROUND INFORMATION

Peer interactions are essential to growth during certain stages of childhood and particularly during adolescence. This is reflected in the psychosocial needs of sick and hospitalized children (Golden, 1983). Infants and children aged 2 to 4 are most susceptible to separation anxiety, so interventions with this age group focus on parent involvement with children. Children aged 4 to 7 are more active with other children, but they are still attached to the significant adults in their lives. Interventions with these children can involve both adults and peers. For the school-age child, interactions with peers may be even more important than interactions with adults since this age group is most concerned with mastery in peer relationships. Adolescents mature by way of their relationships outside of the home, so peers take on even more importance in the process of finding identity and learning how to relate to the opposite sex. For the school-age and adolescent patient, peer group activities are essential therapeutic activities.

Descriptive and formal research documents the effectiveness of group activities for children and adolescents. These group activities have had different goals and participants. British research (Bell, Lyne & Kolvin, 1989) reveals that nondirective group play with economically deprived 5- to 6-year-olds produces short-term decreases in aggressive and regressive play. In their research with preschoolers, Treiber et al. (1985) taught coping skills to a small group of 10 preschoolers about to undergo dental treatment. Compared with a control group, the preschoolers who learned coping skills exhibited less behavioral upset.

Descriptive findings from informal camp activities for school-age children and adolescents (ages 7 through 18 years) with cancer support the positive outcomes of group activities. Based on observations during the camp and afterwards during hospital and/or clinic visits, the residential summer camp experience enabled participants to develop self-confidence and independence, new friendships, a spirit of group identity, and new skills and interests (Shields, Abrams & Siegel, 1985).

Research in Finland with over 2000 14- to 16-year-olds completing questionnaires about social support, life events, and psychosomatic symptoms, reveals that adolescents who lack parental or peer support are at risk for psychosomatic symptoms. This is especially true when the adolescents are experiencing stressful life events (Aro, Hanninen & Paronen, 1989).

Descriptive data also support the benefits of discussion and support groups for hospitalized children and adolescents (Heiney, Ruffin, Ettinger & Ettinger, 1988). Groups of adolescents indicated common themes of concern for participants. Adolescents responded positively to these group interventions; based on these results, more homogeneous groups for chronically ill children and adolescents were developed. Participants in these groups exhibited lower anxiety and increased adaptation to their illness.

SPECIAL CONSIDERATIONS

The first consideration when planning group activities is determining how structured the group will be. The age group and goals of the group are important determinants of this decision. With young children, unstructured play experiences are often more desirable (Bolig, 1986). With older age groups the needs and abilities of the group members can determine whether it is an informal recreational group or a more structured experience, such as a discussion and/or educational group on coping strategies.

Planning is essential for effective structured group activities. Howe and Schwartzberg (1986) describe five considerations in planning and reviewing group interventions: maximum involvement through group-centered actions; maximum sense of individual and group identity; a "flow" experience; spontaneous involvement; and member support and feedback. To achieve maximum involvement through group-centered action, the group planner must consider the group members' levels of functioning and maturity. Activities that enable the participants to be successful should be used. The leader should also present group goals, rules, and expectations. This structure and organization promote group identity. The group activity should occur in a safe environment in which members feel in control of the process. A "flow" experience occurs when group members are functioning effectively at their levels of capability. When the group leader models appropriate skills, the members of the group will be able to model these behaviors spontaneously when they are ready. In a group it is also helpful to have the opportunity for members to offer feedback and support for each other and the group.

ACTIVITY GOALS

The activities in this chapter each focus on a specific task. These events provide some structure and parameters, yet they can be modified to allow more individual or group freedom. The activities have two major goals: to promote social interactions and to encourage exchange of shared feelings among patients.

Social Interaction

Interacting with other patients encourages friendships and support, important coping mechanisms for handling a stressful experience. Activities that promote social interactions are "Autograph Books," "Group Stories," "On Television," "Paper Bag Puppet Show," "Quilt Making," "Hospital Hangman," and "Hospital Pictionary."

Sharing Feelings

When patients acknowledge and share feelings, they can learn that others are feeling the same as they are. This awareness can lead to support and closeness. Activities that encourage the exchange of shared feelings are "Collaborative Proclamations," "Group Mural," "Role Playing," and "Tic Tac Know."

A C T I V I T Y   4 - 1   *AUTOGRAPH BOOKS*

Age Group	7 through 12 years
Patient/Staff Ratio	5:1
Approximate Length	45 minutes
Therapeutic Rationale	To promote social interaction by: • Participating in autograph book making session • Asking staff and other patients to sign the book • Signing books of other patients when asked
Precautions and Restrictions	Participants must have the use of both hands. Check marker, glue, and scissor precautions.
Required Skills	Cutting Pasting Writing
Equipment	Typing paper (5 sheets) Cardboard Scissors Yarn Markers Fabric scraps (optional) Wrapping paper (optional) Paper punch Glue or paste
Implementation	1. Provide each child with 2 pieces of cardboard approximately ½ inch larger than typing paper. 2. Instruct the children to punch three holes on the left-hand side of both pieces of cardboard and the typing paper. Place the typing paper between the two pieces of cardboard. 3. Thread a piece of yarn through each of the three holes and tie in a bow. 4. Decorate the cardboard cover of the book with wrapping paper, markers, and fabric scraps. 5. Ask the children to discuss different ways to use the autograph books, i.e., phone numbers and messages from other patients, messages and autographs from staff. 6. Encourage the children to request autographs from other patients and staff.

A C T I V I T Y 4 - 2

COLLABORATIVE PROCLAMATIONS

Age Group	4 through 12 years
Patient/Staff Ratio:	5:1
Approximate Length	30 minutes

Therapeutic Rationale

To encourage an exchange of shared feelings among patients by:
- Contributing personal feelings to the proclamation
- Discussing feelings and shared experiences with the group (see Fig. 4-1)

Precautions and Restrictions

Participants must have the use of both hands.
Check marker precautions.

Required Skills

Writing

Equipment

Butcher paper or examining table paper (long sheet)
Markers (assorted colors)

Implementation

1. Instruct the group to select a topic. Some possibilities include friendship, hospitalization, illness, happiness, and sadness.
2. Write an open-ended sentence about the topic in large letters on the top of the butcher paper, such as the following:
   Friendship is . . .
   Being in the hospital is like . . .
   I hate being sick because . . .
   Happiness is . . .
   Things that make me sad are . . .
   I am a special person because . . .
3. Have each member of the group complete the sentence and write it below the heading on the butcher paper. Children who are unable to write may dictate their thoughts to someone who will write their words. If the group is small, children may wish to give several statements.
4. Read the proclamation back to the children. Encourage discussion and comments.
5. Hang the proclamation in a prominent place.

A C T I V I T Y 4 - 3	*DISCUSSION GROUPS*

Age Group Adolescence

Patient/Staff Ratio 6:1

Approximate Length 60 minutes

Therapeutic Rationale To encourage an exchange of shared feelings among patients by:
- Participating in a discussion group
- Discussing feelings and shared experiences with the group

Precautions and Restrictions Do not require inhibited or easily threatened adolescents to talk.

Required Skills None

Equipment None

Implementation
1. Gather the adolescents into one room.
2. Have the patients introduce themselves and give a brief explanation about their hospitalization.
3. Have the group suggest a topic of conversation and allow each group member enough time to speak.
4. Encourage openness and social interaction during and after the session.

ACTIVITY 4 - 4   *GROUP MURAL*

Age Group	7 years through adolescence
Patient/Staff Ratio	5:1
Approximate Length	20 minutes

Therapeutic Rationale

To encourage an exchange of shared feelings among patients by:
- Cooperating in the group planning of the mural
- Contributing ideas and suggestions for the mural
- Helping construct the mural
- Discussing the mural when it is finished

Precautions and Restrictions

Participants must have the use of both hands.

Required Skills

Drawing
Coloring

Equipment

Large roll of paper
Markers, crayons, or paint
Pencil

Implementation

1. Preplanning and discussion with the entire group of children is the main focus of this activity. Encourage the group to use the overall theme of illness and/or hospitalization, but allow them to select the specific topic and approach.
2. Have the group sketch the mural with a pencil first, which promotes discussion and allows for changes if desired.
3. When the group is satisfied with the sketch, they may paint or color the mural.
4. When the mural is completed, encourage the group to discuss and critique it. The activity leader should attempt to draw children out and encourage them to express themselves.
5. If possible, the mural should be displayed in a hallway.
6. Encourage staff members to comment on the finished product and give the group positive feedback.

Variation

Cut several types of sponges in 1- to 2-inch squares. Encourage the group to sponge paint the mural.

ACTIVITY 4-5   *GROUP STORIES*

Age Group	10 years through adolescence
Patient/Staff Ratio	10:1
Approximate Length	60 minutes
Therapeutic Rationale	To promote social interaction by: • Contributing suggestions for a story • Participating in story writing activities
Precautions and Restrictions	This activity requires the use of one hand.
Required Skills	Reading Writing
Equipment	Paper Pens or pencils
Implementation	

1. Have the group sit in a circle and select a theme for a story.
2. Provide each participant with a pen and paper.
3. When given a predetermined signal, each child should begin writing a title and paragraph to a story.
4. When the beginning paragraph is completed, the children pass their stories to the left and write a middle paragraph for the story that they have received.
5. Stories are then passed to the right, and those children should add an ending to the story.
6. Each of the stories is read aloud.

| **A C T I V I T Y   4 - 6** | *HOSPITAL HANGMAN* |

Age Group

10 years through adolescence

Patient/Staff Ratio

5:1

Approximate Length

30 minutes

Therapeutic Rationale

To promote social interaction by:
 • Participating in the game until there is a winner

Precautions and Restrictions

Participants must have the use of one hand.
The words selected to play the game should reflect the ability of the players.

Required Skills

Reading
Writing

Equipment

Index cards (4)
Paper for each player
Pencils for each player

Implementation

1. To make the game, write the name of a category on one of the index cards. List the members of that category on the opposite side of the card. Make a card for each category listed.

PERSONNEL	DEPARTMENT	IMPLEMENTS	ILLNESSES
dietician	physical therapy	syringe	pneumonia
nurse	pharmacy	thermometer	fever
doctor	surgery	stethoscope	cancer
lab technician	pediatrics	otoscope	appendicitis
pharmacist	radiology	bandage	tonsillitis

2. To play the game, Player 1 draws an IV pole (instead of gallows) (Fig. 4-2) on his or her paper and selects an index card without letting the other players see. He or she picks one word from the card and on the bottom of the paper makes one dash for each letter of the chosen word.
3. Player 1 should then tell the other players the name of the category on the card. The other players take turns guessing the word, one letter at a time. If a letter is guessed correctly, Player 1 must write it in the correct space or spaces.
4. If a letter is guessed incorrectly, Player 1 draws a portion of a patient connected to the IV pole; head, body, first arm, second arm, first foot, second foot.
5. If a player guesses the word before it is completely filled in, that player wins the round. If Player 1 completes the patient connected to the IV pole, he or she wins.
6. Play continues as described in steps 2 through 5 until all of the players have had two turns.
7. The person having won the most rounds wins the game.

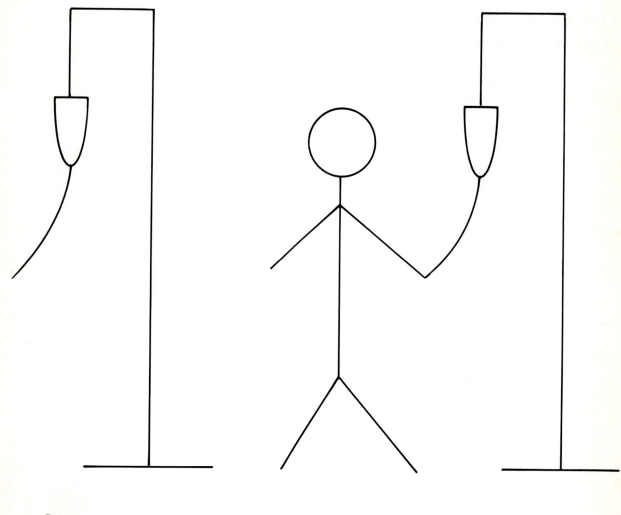

Start   **Finish**

Fig. 4-2

A C T I V I T Y 4 - 7	*HOSPITAL PICTIONARY*

Age Group	10 years through adolescence
Patient/Staff Ratio	8:1
Approximate Length	45 minutes
Therapeutic Rationale	To promote social interaction by: • Participating in the game until one team wins
Precautions and Restrictions	Participants must have the use of one hand.
Required Skills	Reading
Equipment	Index cards (50) Paper Pencils Large drawing pad
Implementation	1. On each of the index cards write three words related to the hospital. Do not use the same word more than once. 2. Divide the players into equal teams and provide each team with paper. 3. Each team selects a member to illustrate. 4. Determine which team will go first. 5. Place the index cards face down on a table. 6. The designated illustrator from the first team draws one card from the pile. 7. The timer is set for 2 minutes and the illustrator draws a picture representing his or her word. Teammates immediately begin trying to guess the word. No writing, verbal cues, or gesturing is allowed during the play. 8. Drawing and guessing stops when the word is guessed or time has run out. 9. Team 2 selects a card and plays as described above. 10. Playing continues until one team has identified three words within the allotted time. That team wins the game.

ACTIVITY 4 - 8   *ON TELEVISION*

Age Group	5 through 10 years
Patient/Staff Ratio	5:1
Approximate Length	60 minutes

Therapeutic Rationale

To promote social interaction by:
- Working with a partner to create a television program
- Acting out their created television show
- Participating in a discussion about the program

Precautions and Restrictions

Check glue and scissor precautions.
Children should be told that only positive comments about the performance will be expressed.

Required Skills

Cutting
Pasting

Equipment

Cardboard box (large enough to accommodate at least two children)
Woodgrain contact paper
Cups
Empty toilet paper tube
Scissors
Glue

Implementation

1. Assist the children in cutting out a hole in the box to make the television screen.
2. Cover the box with contact paper.
3. Glue paper cups to the box to represent dials.
4. Divide the children into two groups.
5. Discuss different types of television programs.
6. Suggest to the children that they use a hospital theme for their television show.
7. Give the children time to discuss what they want to do for their performance.
8. Have each group get "into" the television set and act out their show, using the toilet paper roll as a microphone.
9. After each group has finished, allow time for discussion. Encourage children to give positive feedback by asking what they liked about the show. Encourage the children to share feelings and experiences related to the theme of the skit.

A C T I V I T Y 4 - 9	*PAPER BAG PUPPET SHOW*

Age Group	5 through 12 years
Patient/Staff Ratio	5:1
Approximate Length	60 minutes
Therapeutic Rationale	To promote social interaction by: • Contributing to the selection of a theme or story on which to base a puppet show • Assisting in the construction of puppets • Participating in the puppet show performance
Precautions and Restrictions	Participants need the use of both hands. Check glue and scissor precautions.
Required Skills	Cutting Pasting
Equipment	Small paper bags Construction paper Scissors Paste
Implementation	1. Have the group select a theme or story on which to base their puppet show. 2. Discuss what type of characters will be needed, and have each child select a character to make. 3. Cut the puppet features, clothing, and extremities out of construction paper. 4. Paste construction paper cutouts onto the paper bag. 5. Allow the group sufficient time to discuss and rehearse their puppet show. 6. Have the group perform the puppet show for the staff and/or other children. Provide the group with positive feedback for their efforts.

ACTIVITY 4-10   *QUILT MAKING*

Age Group   8 years through adolescence

Patient/Staff Ratio   5:1

Approximate Length   60 minutes

Therapeutic Rationale   To promote social interaction by:
- Contributing to preplanning discussion and selection of theme for quilt
- Assisting in the construction of quilt squares
- Participating in conversation with other group members while assembling the quilt

Precautions and Restrictions   This activity requires the use of both hands.
Follow institution's guidelines for the disposal of needles. Usually specific containers are indicated into which needles are placed to prevent injury.

Required Skills   Sewing

Equipment   White cotton squares (8 inches each)
Fabric paint
Quilt batting
Yarn
Thread
Disposable needles

Implementation
1. Preplanning and discussion with the entire group of children is the main focus of this activity. Allow the children to select the subject or the theme of the quilt.
2. Give each child two fabric squares (Fig. 4-3).
3. Have each child decorate one square, using fabric paint.
4. With wrong sides together, stitch a decorated fabric to an undecorated square. Leave an area about 2 inches long unstitched.
5. Turn the fabric squares inside out and stuff lightly with quilt batting.
6. Slip stitch the 2-inch opening closed.
7. Using yarn, make a knot in the middle of each square. Bring the yarn down through the front and up through the back. Cut the ends about 1 inch from the quilt.
8. Sew squares together to form quilt.

Steps 2 & 3

Step 4a

Step 4b

Step 5

Step 6

Step 7a

Step 7b

Step 8

Fig. 4-3

A C T I V I T Y 4 - 1 1   *ROLE PLAYING*

Age Group	6 through 10 years
Patient/Staff Ratio	5:1
Approximate Length	20 minutes
Therapeutic Rationale	To encourage an exchange of shared feelings by: • Contributing to discussion about role play pictures • Participating in role play activities
Precautions and Restrictions	None
Required Skills	None

Equipment	Pictures from magazines and other sources mounted on cardboard
	Pictures should depict such situations as:
	  Child having blood drawn
	  Child being examined by medical personnel
	  Crying child being comforted by a nurse
	  Angry child
	Assorted appropriate props:
	  Syringes without needles
	  Lab coat
	  Stethoscope

Implementation	1. Divide the children into small groups of two or three each. 2. Place pictures face down and have a representative of each group select a picture. 3. Have the groups discuss what is happening in the picture, including what the people are feeling and saying. 4. Allow the groups to select props. 5. Have the groups, one at a time, act out the situation on the card. Encourage them to expand on what they see in the picture. 6. After each group has finished, allow time for discussion. Each child should have an opportunity to comment on similar experiences he or she has encountered.

ACTIVITY 4-12	*TIC TACK KNOW*

Age Group	8 years through adolescence
Patient/Staff Ratio	5:1
Approximate Length	20 minutes
Therapeutic Rationale	To encourage an exchange of shared feelings by: • Requesting other patients and staff members to "fill in" the Tic Tac Know boxes • Finding three patients with a common factor, e.g., similar interest, illness
Precautions and Restrictions	Check marker precautions. Participants must have use of one hand. Children must be advised of rooms that they cannot enter.
Required Skills	Reading Writing
Equipment	Paper Marker Pen or pencil
Implementation	1. Make Tic Tac Know sheets by drawing two vertical lines and two horizontal lines dividing each sheet of paper into nine boxes. 2. In each box write a task that will require the child to converse with other children. These may include: find another child who has the same favorite singing group, find another child who has undergone the same test or procedure, find another child whose birthday falls in the same month. 3. Give each child participating a Tic Tac Know sheet. 4. Instruct participants to find a person who fits the description in each of the Tic Tac Know boxes. 5. Patients who match the description in the box should sign the box. 6. The first patient with three signatures in a row wins the game.

ADDITIONAL IDEAS

- Sponsor tournaments; backgammon, checkers, chess, or Monopoly work well.
- Adolescents may enjoy participating on a debating team.
- Serve "high tea" at 4:00 PM in the playroom.
- Form committees to do certain tasks or plan events, such as decorating the playroom or deciding the activity for the afternoon.
- Have an ethnic food feast! Patients can create the menu and prepare the food. Decorate the playroom to reflect the theme and play folk tunes of the selected nationality.

- Give parties to celebrate obscure holidays, celebrity birthdays, or dubiously important events. The following are some ideas that have worked well:
- Chinese New Year (varies between January 21 and February 19)
- April Fool's Day (April 1)
- National Hot Dog Month (July 1-31)
- Ground Hog Day (February 2)
- Children's Day (second Sunday in June)

REFERENCES

Aro, H., Hanninen, V., & Paronen, O. (1989). Social support, life events and psychosomatic symptoms among 14-16-year-old adolescents. *Social Science Medicine, 29* (9), 1051-1056.

Bell, V., Lyne, S., & Kolvin, I. (1989). Playgroup therapy with deprived children: Community-based early secondary prevention. *British Journal of Occupational Therapy, 52* (12), 458-462.

Bolig, R. (Ed.). (1986). Unstructured play in hospital settings: An internal locus of control rationale. *Children's Health Care, 15* (2), 101-107.

Golden, D.B. (1983). Play therapy for hospitalized children. In C.E. Schaefer & K.J. O'Connor (Eds.), *Handbook of play therapy* (pp. 213-233). New York: John Wiley & Sons.

Heiney, S.P., Ruffin, J., Ettinger, R.S., & Ettinger, S. (1988). The effects of group therapy on adolescents with cancer. *Journal of the Association of Pediatric Oncology Nurses, 5* (3), 20-24.

Howe, M.C. & Schwartzberg, S.L. (1986). *A functional approach to group work in occupational therapy.* Philadelphia: J.B. Lippincott.

Shields, J.M., Abrams, P., & Siegel, S. (1985). An alternative health care setting for children with cancer: A residential summer camp. *Children's Health Care, 13* (3), 135-138.

Treiber, F.A., Seidner, A.L., Lee, A.A., Morgan, S.A., & Jackson, J. (1985). Effects of a group cognitive-behavioral treatment on preschool children's responses to dental treatment. *Children's Health Care, 13* (3), 117-121.

CHAPTER 5

EXPRESSIVE ARTS WITH MEDICAL EQUIPMENT ACTIVITIES

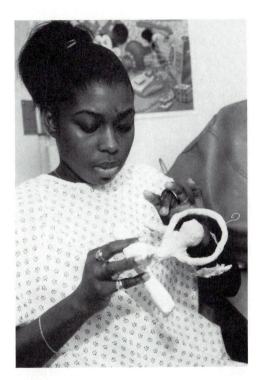

Fig. 5-1 Casting bandage constructions.

This chapter contains expressive art activities with medical equipment as the medium for expression. The activities can be used when children are too anxious or afraid to engage in more formal types of medical play or preparation. Expressive art activities are also useful when children feel they are "too old" for medical play. The activities use indirect and sometimes humorous ways to expose children to medical equipment. This form of medical play is a useful supplement to other medical play and preparation activities.

BACKGROUND INFORMATION

McCue (1988) states that medical play is a distinct concept within the phenomenon of play. It is a form of play that always involves medical themes or medical equipment. An adult or child can initiate medical play, but the child chooses to maintain it voluntarily. This type of play is often accompanied by laughter and relaxation but can also be intense and aggressive. Medical play is not synonymous with preparation since it does not involve an adult demonstrating a procedure or familiarizing a child in a formal educational manner.

McCue (1988) defines four types of medical play: role rehearsal/role reversal medical play, medical fantasy play, indirect medical play, and medical art. The activities in this chapter are examples of medical art. McCue extends medical art to include all types of art materials, including medical equipment, used in both representational and nonrepresentational ways. While McCue believes that either the process or the product of the activity can be important for the child, art therapists emphasize that the process or the experience is what counts, not the product (Walker, 1989). Art therapists use various media, such as painting, drawing, or sculpting, to allow people to understand themselves, their feelings, and their relationships. These artistic efforts enable conflicts to be worked through, channeled, and resolved, all without the use of words. The objectives of art therapy include widening the range of communication, inviting exploratory learning, providing tasks that are self-rewarding, and reinforcing emotional balance (Johnson & Berendts, 1986; Trent, 1986). No matter what the art medium, the child can express himself kinesthetically, affectively, cognitively, symbolically, and/or creatively (Walker, 1989).

Children obtain helpful exposure to medical equipment when it is used in expressive arts activities. Their knowledge and understanding of medical equipment increases with age in a manner best described by the Piagetian theoretical framework (Brewster, 1982; Perrin & Gerrity, 1981; Redpath & Rogers, 1984; Siaw, Stephens & Holmes, 1986; Thompson, 1985). Age-appropriate opportunities to manipulate and use medical equipment in a nonstressful situation like medical art can assist in this learning process.

Research also indicates that children who have higher anxiety levels have less knowledge about equipment and procedures (Melamed, 1982; Siaw, Stephens & Holmes, 1986; Thompson, 1985). There is some indication that children who play with hospital-related toys before hospitalization report less anxiety and distress than those who do not (Burstein & Meichenbaum, 1979); however, more research must be done to further document these findings.

Other relevant research with chronically ill children reveals that children are able to use medical equipment to express their concerns about intrusive procedures (Ellerton, Caty & Ritchie, 1985). Injection play was the most common type of intrusive procedure acted out in this research.

An important part of this play was exploratory. Children first picked up the needle and syringe, examined them, and worked the plunger back and forth before acting out the intrusive procedure. Less intrusive and anxiety-provoking equipment produced less exploratory activities. These findings indicate that exploratory opportunities via medical art can help children familiarize themselves with medical equipment before or after role rehearsal/role reversal medical play and medical fantasy play occur.

SPECIAL CONSIDERATIONS

One of the first considerations when doing medical art with children is the role of the adult. Should the adult be actively involved in the project or a passive observer? Bolig, Fernie & Klein (1986) state that unstructured play without adult guidance offers the greatest opportunities for children to gain skills and achieve mastery. When play is inhibited because of immobility, dull or repetitious environments, overstimulating environments, or fear, then adults may need to take on a more active role in the medical play of the child (Crocker, 1978). The amount of involvement and control of the adult should be carefully considered when conducting medical play (McCue, 1988).

Another consideration in medical play is the type of equipment selected. Commercial equipment can be costly, but McCue (1988) notes that good medical play can also occur with simple materials available in the hospital (e.g., cotton, bandage strips, syringes).

During medical art play the activities of the child may not be directly interpretable. McCue (1988) suggests that you ask a child, "Were you thinking of anything special while you were . . . ?" rather than, "What is it?" The child is more likely to respond and provide meaningful information to the professional.

ACTIVITY GOALS

All of the activities in this chapter have the same goal—to enable children to explore informally and use medical equipment to express themselves in art. The activities use a variety of materials. We hope that they will stimulate you to create your own variations, as well as new activities.

A C T I V I T Y 5 - 1	*CASTED HANDS*

Age Group	5 through 14
Patient/Staff Ratio	5:1
Approximate Length	Two 20-minute sessions
Therapeutic Rationale	Participates in art activities with medical implements by:

Participates in art activities with medical implements by:
- Using medical implements in nonthreatening art activities
- Constructing original design with medical implements

Gains mastery over medical implements by:
- Exploring and manipulating medical implements
- Using the activity as a vehicle to identify, explore, and discuss experiences and feelings associated with the implements

Precautions and Restrictions

This activity requires the use of both hands.
Children may require assistance with inflating the glove and tying off the opening with a rubber band.
Check scissor precautions.

Required Skills

Cutting

Equipment

Casting bandages
Small basin filled with warm water
Surgical glove
Scissors
Rubber band
Paint
Brushes

Implementation

1. Instruct the children to cut the casting bandages into 1-inch strips.
2. While the children are cutting casting bandage strips, inflate the surgical glove and knot the end or tie it with a rubber band.
3. Have the children wet one bandage strip and apply it to the inflated glove. Repeat, overlapping the strips slightly, until the glove is completely covered with two layers of strips.
4. Smooth the surface with your fingers throughout the procedure, wiping off any excess plaster.
5. Allow the glove to dry, and paint or decorate as desired.
6. Discuss materials and product with younger children. With older children discuss the process of casting.

A C T I V I T Y 5 - 2	*CASTING BANDAGE CONSTRUCTIONS**

Age Group 8 years through adolescence

Patient/Staff Ratio 5:1

Approximate Length Two 45 to 60 minute sessions

Therapeutic Rationale Participates in art activities with medical implements by:
- Using medical implements in nonthreatening art activities
- Constructing original design with medical implements

Gains mastery over medical implements by:
- Exploring and manipulating medical implements
- Using the activity as a vehicle to identify, explore, and discuss experiences and feelings associated with the implements

Precautions and Restrictions Requires the use of both hands.
IV sites and open wound on hands need to be protected from plaster.

Required Skills None

Equipment Casting bandage
Foil or pliable wire
Paint
Brushes
Shallow bowl filled with warm water
Masking tape (if using foil)

Implementation
1. Make armature (underlying structure using wire or crumpled foil strengthened with masking tape).
2. Cut casting bandage into strips. The length of the strips should be a manageable size for the armature.
3. Dip the strips into water and apply to the armature. Continue until the entire armature is covered with two or three layers of strips.
4. Allow to dry well.
5. Paint the construction and decorate as desired.

---

*Contributed by Leigh Merrinew

A C T I V I T Y 5 - 5	*FIVE FINGER PUPPETS*

Age Group	4 through 10 years
Approximate Length	15 minutes
Patient/Staff Ratio	5:1
Therapeutic Rationale	Participates in art activities with medical implements by: • Using medical implements in nonthreatening art activities • Constructing original design with medical implements Gains mastery over medical implements by: • Exploring and manipulating medical implements • Using the activity as a vehicle to identify, explore, and discuss experiences and feelings associated with the implements
Precautions and Restrictions	Check marker, glue, and scissor precautions. This activity requires the use of both hands. Care should be taken so that children who have any respiratory conditions do not inhale vapors from the fixative.
Required Skills	Cutting Pasting
Equipment	Examining glove Markers Yarn Scissors Glue Cotton Fixative or hair spray
Implementation	1. Stuff each finger of the examining glove with a cottonball. 2. Place the glove on the child's nondominant hand. 3. Have the child use his or her dominant hand to draw figures on each finger of the glove. Spray the glove with a fixative. 4. If desired, have the child remove the glove and glue yarn on each of the finger tips for hair. 5. Encourage the child to speak through the puppet.

ACTIVITY 5-6	*FOIL ART*

Age Group	10 years through adolescence
Patient/Staff Ratio	5:1
Approximate Length	60 minutes
Therapeutic Rationale	Participates in art activities with medical implements by: • Using medical implements in nonthreatening art activities • Constructing original design with medical implements Gains mastery over medical implements by: • Exploring and manipulating medical implements • Using the activity as a vehicle to identify, explore, and discuss experiences and feelings associated with the implements
Precautions and Restrictions	Check glue and scissor precautions. This activity requires the use of both hands.
Required Skills	Cutting Pasting

Equipment	Assorted hospital implements: Small cup or can
	   uncontaminated IV tubing Brushes
	   tongue depressors Scissors
	   gauze pads White glue
	   safety pins Heavy cardboard
	   cotton swab sticks India ink or tempera paint
	Heavy aluminum foil Tourniquet tubing

Implementation

1. Instruct each child to plan a design or picture using hospital implements. Glue them in place on heavy cardboard. Allow the glue to dry completely.
2. While the child is implementing step 1, the activity leader should mix two parts of glue with one part of water in a small container. Paint this glue over the whole surface of the cardboard, including the hospital implements.
3. Have each child cut a piece of aluminum foil about 1½ inches larger than the cardboard on all sides.
4. Instruct them to lay the foil over the surface of the design, gently molding the foil to the surface, pressing it around the object so the shape and texture can be seen.
5. Fold the edges of the foil behind the cardboard, and secure them with tape or glue.
6. Paint the entire surface of the picture with India ink or tempera paint.
7. When the picture is dry, gently polish the surface with a soft cloth to create an antique effect.

ACTIVITY 5-7   *GAUZE SOFT SCULPTURE*

Age Group	7 years through adolescence
Patient/Staff Ratio	5:1
Approximate Length	30 minutes
Therapeutic Rationale	Participates in art activities with medical implements by: • Using medical implements in nonthreatening art activities • Constructing original design with medical implements Gains mastery over medical implements by: • Exploring and manipulating medical implements • Using the activity as a vehicle to identify, explore, and discuss experiences and feelings associated with the implements
Precautions and Restrictions	Participants need to have the use of both hands. This activity requires supervision when using straight pins. Pins should be disposed of when activity is completed. Check glue and scissor precautions.
Required Skills	Cutting Sewing Drawing and tracing

Equipment

Large gauze pads   Pencil
Large plastic darning needle   Fabric scraps
Scissors   Glue
Yarn   Paper
Pins   Cottonballs

Implementation

1. Instruct the children to make a pattern by drawing an outline of an object, person, or shape on a piece of paper.
2. Have them cut the outline to make a pattern.
3. Place two gauze pads together, matching all four corners. Pin the pattern to the gauze pads and cut it out.
4. The children may decorate the shape with fabric scraps and yarn. Decorations may be sewn or glued to the gauze.
5. Thread the darning needle with yarn and sew pieces of gauze together, leaving a 2-inch opening.
6. Stuff cottonballs through the opening, making sure it reaches all corners.
7. Sew the opening closed.

Variation

Bean bags may be made by substituting dried beans for cottonballs.
Cut ice skate shapes from large gauze pads. Attach paper clips for ice skate, decorate with glitter, and use as a Christmas tree ornament.
During the Halloween season have the children construct gauze ghosts.

A C T I V I T Y 5 - 8	*HOSPITAL PRINTING*

Age Group 3 through 10 years

Patient/Staff Ratio 5:1

Approximate Length 20 minutes

Therapeutic Rationale Participates in art activities with medical implements by:
- Using medical implements in nonthreatening art activities
- Constructing original design with medical implements

Gains mastery over medical implements by:
- Exploring and manipulating medical implements
- Using the activity as a vehicle to identify, explore, and discuss experiences and feelings associated with the implements

Precautions and Restrictions This activity requires the use of one hand.

Required Skills None

Equipment Assorted expendable supplies:
    syringes with needles
    leads
    specimen cups
    tongue depressors
    cotton-tip applicators
    oral swabs
    plastic medication cups
Tempera paints
Shallow dishes
Paper

Implementation
1. Pour small amounts of tempera paint into shallow dishes.
2. Dip various implements in the paint and "print" on the paper, making designs.

Variation Fold the paper in half. Place a paint-soaked object on one half of the paper and remove it, leaving a print. Fold the paper again and rub your hand across the paper to create a "Rorschach." Have each child discuss his or her picture.

A C T I V I T Y 5 - 9	*HOSPITAL RUBBINGS*

Age Group   3 through 7 years

Patient/Staff Ratio   5:1

Approximate Length   15 minutes

Therapeutic Rationale   Participates in art activities with medical implements by:
- Using medical implements in nonthreatening art activities
- Constructing original design with medical implements

Gains mastery over medical implements by:
- Exploring and manipulating medical implements
- Using the activity as a vehicle to identify, explore, and discuss experiences and feelings associated with the implements

Precautions and Restrictions   Participants must have the use of both hands.

Required Skills   Coloring

Equipment   Assortment of hospital implements with interesting shapes such as:
    bandages
    flattened paper medicine cups
    tongue depressors
Dustless colored chalk or crayons
Thin paper

Implementation
1. Place an implement on the table for each child.
2. Have the children place a piece of paper over the implement and rub hard over the surface with a crayon or chalk.

Variation   Letters may be cut out of cardboard spelling the child's name or name of the implements used. Rubbings may then be made using the letters.
Make cardboard representations of hospital implements to use in place of actual equipment.

ACTIVITY 5-10   *HOSPITAL SANDCASTING*

Age Group	10 years through adolescence
Patient/Staff Ratio	5:1
Approximate Length	Two 30-minute sessions

Therapeutic Rationale

Participates in art activities with medical implements by:
- Using medical implements in nonthreatening art activities
- Constructing original design with medical implements

Gains mastery over medical implements by:
- Exploring and manipulating medical implements
- Using the activity as a vehicle to identify, explore, and discuss experiences and feelings associated with the implements

Precautions and Restrictions

Children with IVs or open wounds on their hands or arms should not participate.

The activity can be messy and should be well supervised.

Participants must have the use of one hand.

Required Skills

None

Equipment

Small expendable supplies
   IV tubing
   syringes without needles
   medicine cups
Sturdy cardboard box filled with 5 inches of sand
Water
Plaster of Paris (5 pounds)

Implementation

1. Pour enough water into the box to dampen the sand so the grains stick together.
2. Have the children press the implements into the sand mold until they are halfway submerged. Remove the implement from the sand leaving the implement shape intact, forming the mold for the cast.
3. Mix the Plaster of Paris according to the package directions.
4. Have the children pour the plaster into the mold, filling it just to the edge.
5. Allow the plaster to harden completely.
6. Remove the cast and gently rinse off any remaining sand.
7. Allow the children to decorate their sandcast.

A C T I V I T Y 5 - 1 3	***SPATTER PAINTING WITH HOSPITAL EQUIPMENT***

Age Group — 7 years through adolescence

Patient/Staff Ratio — 5:1

Approximate Length — 20 minutes

Therapeutic Rationale — Participates in art activities with medical implements by:
- Using medical implements in nonthreatening art activities
- Constructing original design with medical implements

Gains mastery over medical implements by:
- Exploring and manipulating medical implements
- Using the activity as a vehicle to identify, explore, and discuss experiences and feelings associated with the implements

Precautions and Restrictions — Participants must have the use of both hands.

Required Skills — None

Equipment —
Paper
Expendable hospital supplies (variety)
Toothbrush
Tape
Tempera paint (thin)
Firm piece of wire screen affixed to a frame of heavy cardboard or wood
Colored construction paper
Masking tape

Implementation —
1. Have each child arrange the objects on a sheet of paper, and secure it with a small piece of tape.
2. Instruct the child to dip a toothbrush in the thinned tempera paint, tapping off any extra paint.
3. Have the child hold the screen 3 to 5 inches from the paper. Quickly rub the paint-soaked brush back and forth over the screen.
4. When the paint has dried, remove the implements from the paper and mount the art on a piece of contrasting construction paper.

A C T I V I T Y 5 - 1 4	*SPECIMEN CUP BANK*

Age Group	5 through 8 years
Patient/Staff Ratio	5:1
Approximate Length	15 minutes
Therapeutic Rationale	Participates in art activities with medical implements by: • Using medical implements in nonthreatening art activities • Constructing original design with medical implements Gains mastery over medical implements by: • Exploring and manipulating medical implements • Using the activity as a vehicle to identify, explore, and discuss experiences and feelings associated with the implements
Precautions and Restrictions	This activity requires the use of both hands. Check glue and scissor precautions.
Required Skills	Cutting Pasting
Equipment	Plastic specimen cup Paper and/or fabric scraps Scissors Glue Single-edged razor blade
Implementation	1. Before the activity session, use the razor blade to make a slit (large enough for coins to pass through) in the lid of the specimen cup. 2. Screw the lid tightly onto the cup. 3. Allow the children to decorate the bank as they choose, using paper and fabric scraps.

A C T I V I T Y 5 - 1 5

SPECIMEN CUP SAND ART

Age Group
6 years through adolescence

Patient/Staff Ratio
5:1

Approximate Length
45 minutes

Therapeutic Rationale
Participates in art activities with medical implements by:
- Using medical implements in nonthreatening art activities
- Constructing original design with medical implement

Gains mastery over medical implements by:
- Exploring and manipulating medical implements
- Using the activity as a vehicle to identify, explore, and discuss experiences and feelings associated with the implements

Precautions and Restrictions
Children must have the use of one hand.
Children who might ingest the sand must be closely supervised.

Required Skills
None

Equipment
Clear specimen cups with lids or formula bottles
Assorted colors of terrarium sand or aquarium gravel
Tongue depressor
Small medicine cups

Implementation
1. Instruct children to use medicine cups to dip into sand and pour approximately one-half inch of sand into a specimen cup.
2. Have them pour a second layer of a different color on top of the first layer.
3. Use a tongue depressor to create designs in the sand. Place the tongue depressor along the inside edge of the cup. Move it up and down to push the sand into the desired pattern.
4. Continue to fill the specimen cup with colored sand until the container is completely full.
5. Have the children cover the sand with a thin layer of glue and place the specimen cup cap back on the container.

Variation
Use corn meal and cookie decorating sparkles instead of sand for children who are known to ingest inedible substances.
Salt mixed with powdered tempera paint may be substituted for colored terrarium sand.
Salt may also be colored by rubbing a piece of colored chalk over a tea strainer for several minutes and mixing the chalk dust with the salt.

A C T I V I T Y   5 -

Age Gro

Patient/Staff Ra

Approximate Len

Therapeutic Ration

Precautions
Restricti

Required Sl

Equipm

Implementa

Varia

A C T I V I T Y   5 - 1 6

Age Group

Patient/Staff Ratio

Approximate Length

Therapeutic Rationale

Precautions and
Restrictions

Required Skills

Equipment

Implementation

SYRINGE PENCIL CASE

10 through 14 years

5:1

40 minutes

Participates in art activities with medical implements by:
- Using hospital implements in a nonthreatening art activity
- Facilitates discussion about shots

Children will require supervision and assistance when using the needle.
This activity requires the use of both hands.

Cutting

Syringe (50 ml)
Glue
Crayon
Scissors
String
Button
Needle
Paper

1. Remove the plunger from the barrel of the syringe.
2. Remove the rubber tip from the plunger.
3. Using a large-gauge sewing needle, make a hole in the point of the rubber tip and pass a short piece of string through it (Fig. 5-2).
4. Make a knot on the underside of the rubber tip, leaving 1½ inches of string. Attach a button and knot it; this will be the cap to the pencil case.
5. Decorate the barrel of the syringe using crayons and paper scraps.
6. Place the rubber tip on the tube with the pointed end facing inward.

Button

Stopper

A child with a strong sense of self-worth is more likely to have the confidence to develop new coping mechanisms, make positive adjustments to change, and capably handle stress. Fostering self-esteem is therefore an important psychosocial goal for the pediatric health care professional. The activities in this chapter are designed to help meet this goal. Additional activities addressing self-expression, body image, and group interactions are in other chapters to supplement those in this chapter.

BACKGROUND INFORMATION

Self-esteem is one of the most important personal resources a child can possess to deal effectively with the world. It is the basis for personal growth and healthy development (Winkelstein, 1989), and some believe that it is the single most important factor affecting behavior (Miller, 1987). Professionals agree that self-esteem is part of a complex process involved in the child's and adult's mental pictures of themselves. These mental pictures include ideas, beliefs, and attitudes about the self (self-concept), thoughts and feelings about physical appearance (body image), and self-worth (self-esteem) (Crosby, 1982). It is difficult to separate self-concept, self-esteem, and body image (Stanwyck, 1983).

The child's self-esteem develops from birth. During infancy children learn about themselves from physical growth, cognitive development, and observations of the reactions of others. Throughout childhood, adolescence, and adulthood, self-esteem is influenced and developed through interactions with others and the feedback obtained from parents, teachers, role models, and friends (Meisenhelder, 1985).

Four elements of life experience affect the development of self-esteem: significant others, social role expectations, psychosocial development crisis, and family communication/coping style (Stanwyck, 1983). As the child's world expands, so do the opportunities to change or expand the circle of significant others in his life. Significant others communicate messages to the child about himself in relation to cultural, familial, and other social role expectations. Whether the child or adolescent chooses to follow these role expectations can affect self-esteem. In addition, the psychosocial crises defined by Erikson (1950, 1968) affect

the child's self-esteem. Successfully negotiating the developmental crisis of each age period results in a better understanding and acceptance of self and subsequent self-worth. The communication and coping styles within families also affect how children deal with stress. A child growing up in a dysfunctional family learns coping behaviors that may be harmful for the child's evolving self-esteem.

Recent research documents the relationship between positive self-concept and pediatric health (Beier, 1981; Leonardson, 1986; Meisenhelder, 1985). Negative self-concept is related to self-destructive health behaviors such as overeating, alcoholism, smoking, and drug abuse in children and adolescents (Klos, 1986; Papenfuss et al, 1983). Research also indicates that hospitalization can lower the self-esteem of older school-aged children (Riffee, 1981).

Interventions to promote self-esteem have been successfully used with both healthy and sick children (Hamachek, 1980; Popka, 1980; Reasoner, 1983). These interventions have addressed five basic attitudes in the child (Reasoner, 1983): a sense of security, a sense of identity or self-concept, a sense of belonging, a sense of purpose, and a sense of personal competence.

Hospitalized children gain a sense of security by feeling they can trust and have confidence in the adults responsible for them. Meisenhelder (1985) emphasizes the importance of the health care professional as the significant other in the life experience of the patient, especially in health care settings where there is high contact, such as in intensive or extended care units. Children also gain a sense of security when significant others tell them (in age-appropriate ways) what things will be happening to them and what is expected of them.

To promote a sense of identity, children need to have positive feedback and recognition of their strengths. They need encouragement to evaluate their own strengths and weaknesses in order to better help themselves. All of these interventions must be done while demonstrating love and acceptance.

A sense of belonging is an important step in building self-esteem, especially among adolescents. To accomplish this goal, children and adolescents need experiences that enable them to realize when it is appropriate to be a unique individual and when it is important to identify with and be a part of a group.

A sense of purpose can be promoted by setting reasonable expectations for children while helping them set realistic goals for themselves. We can then communicate faith and confidence that they will achieve their goals. Health care professionals can also encourage children to expand their interests, skills, and talents even while they are ill.

Finally, a sense of personal competence is achieved when the child believes that he or she is able to cope with problems or meet goals. A sense of personal competence evolves with successful experiences. We can assist children by helping them choose from options available, providing encouragement and support, and offering feedback regarding their progress. Research indicates that increased feelings of self-efficacy are associated with greater self-management behavior in chronically ill children (Clark et al, 1988).

SPECIAL CONSIDERATIONS

The availability of significant others as well as their interactions with the child are important variables affecting self-esteem. Considering the child's psychosocial stage can help us know who these significant others are (Miller, 1987). Health care providers can become significant others in the life of the sick child and facilitate patient contact with close family and friends. They can also coordinate successful transitions from a health care environment into the home, school, and community (Meisenhelder, 1985).

Nonverbal communication of significant others provides powerful feedback to the child and can affect self-esteem. Facial expressions, body language, and voice tones can indicate care, concern, and respect for the child and subsequently influence self-esteem (Meisenhelder, 1985).

In an environment of positive support and openness, self-esteem is promoted, children have opportunities to make choices and decisions, and competition is avoided while cooperation is encouraged.

ACTIVITY GOALS

The activities in this chapter are designed to enhance self-esteem by focusing on the child's sense of identity and uniqueness or his personal strengths and accomplishments.

Sense of Identity and Uniqueness

Activities that incorporate the child's name, such as "Caterpillar Name Plaque," "Decorative Name Bracelet," "Magazine Name Collages," and "Photo Necklace" promote a sense of identity. Creating "Casting Bandage Masks" and "Fingerprint Forms" also helps children appreciate their uniqueness. Encourage children to display their finished products to personalize their own space.

Personal Strengths and Accomplishments

The ill child is challenged to find effective means for dealing with a stressful experience. "Can Do Hands," "Guess Who Game," "Name Poems," "Personal Collages," "Very Important Patient Posters," and "Personalized Pennants" can help the child focus on personal strengths and accomplishments.

ACTIVITY 6-1   *CAN DO HANDS*

Age Group	5 through 7 years
Patient/Staff Ratio	3:1
Approximate Length	15 minutes
Therapeutic Rationale	To foster self-esteem by: • Describing individual strengths
Precautions and Restrictions	Children must have the use of both hands. Younger children will need assistance cutting. Check marker, glue, and scissor precautions.
Required Skills	Cutting Pasting
Equipment	Construction paper Marker Paste or glue Scissors
Implementation	1. Trace an outline of the hands of each child onto construction paper. Be sure the fingers are spread. 2. Have the children cut out their hand outline. 3. Discuss with the children things they can do with their hands. 4. Write one thing they can do on each of the 10 fingers. 5. Paste the hands on a contrasting color of construction paper. 6. To further promote self-esteem, hang the hands in a prominent place and encourage staff members and parents to give the child positive feedback.
Variation	Have the children trace their hands several times on green construction paper and cut them out. Arrange and glue the hands on a posterboard cut in the shape of a wreath. Use a hand cut from brown construction paper to create a Thanksgiving turkey. Just add legs, a wattle, and features.

ACTIVITY 6-2   *CASTING BANDAGE MASKS*

Age Group	6 years through adolescence
Patient/Staff Ratio	3:1
Approximate Length	30 minutes per mask
Therapeutic Rationale	To foster self-esteem by: • Distinguishing unique individual characteristics

Precautions and Restrictions

Some children may be frightened of having their entire face covered with plaster casting material and should not be forced to participate.

Children must cover their entire face with petroleum jelly, so check for allergies.

This activity should not be used with children whose skin may be sensitive to the casting material or who have burns, lacerations, open cuts, or incisions on their face.

Check scissors precaution.

Do not apply casting material directly to the skin.

Apply acrylic sealer in a well-ventilated area. It may be hazardous for children with certain conditions (e.g., asthma) and should not be applied in their presence.

Required Skills   Cutting

Equipment

Long table	Scissors
Towels	Petroleum jelly
Basin	Paint
Water	Spray acrylic sealer
Gauze pads (4″ × 4″)	Brushes
Plaster casting bandages	Blow dryer

Implementations

1. Have the children cut nose-size triangles from the casting bandages.
2. Instruct one child to lie on the table. Cover his or her face with petroleum jelly.
3. Cut two eye-size pieces from a gauze pad. Place them over the child's eyes (Fig. 6-2).
4. Dip two triangles in the basin filled with water and place them over the child's nose. The casting bandage works best if it is twofold.
5. Continue to work on the nose area until the nose and upper lip are completely covered. A rectangle cut the size of the upper lip works well.
6. Cover the rest of the face with large pieces of twofold casting bandages, gently pressing on the facial features so that they impress into the casting bandage.
7. Let the mask dry 10 minutes and remove it from the child's face. Drying time can be expedited by using a hair dryer.
8. Trim uneven edges with casting bandage shears.
9. Allow the child to decorate the mask when it has dried. When the paint has dried, spray the mask with acrylic sealer.

Variation   Have the children create masks for Halloween.

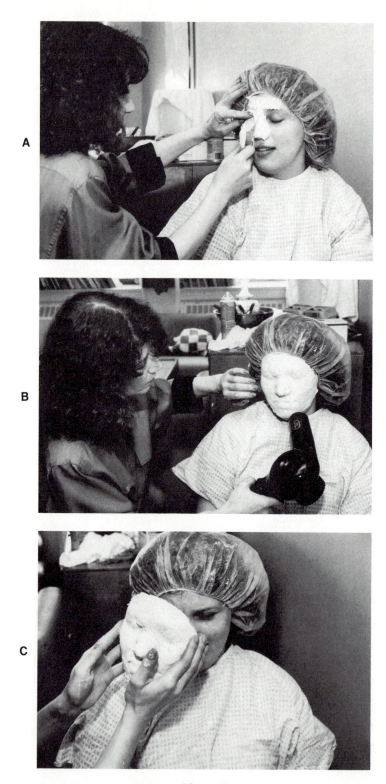

Fig. 6-2

ACTIVITY 6-3 — *CATERPILLAR NAME PLAQUE*

Age Group 5 through 8 years

Patient/Staff Ratio 5:1

Approximate Length 60 minutes

Therapeutic Rationale To foster self-esteem by:
- Distinguishing individual characteristics

Precautions and Restrictions Children must have the use of both hands.
Check marker, glue, and scissor precautions.

Required Skills Pasting
The participants must be able to write their names.

Equipment Metal caps, such as baby food jar lids
Scissors
Markers
Glue
Tempera paint
Paint brush
Construction paper
Pipe cleaners
Spring clothespin

Implementation

1. Give each child as many caps as there are letters in his or her name, plus one extra cap for the caterpillar's head.
2. Mix the tempera paint with a small amount of glue and paint all of the caps.
3. Cut the caterpillar's features from construction paper and glue them on a cap to be the head (Fig. 6-3).
4. Form the pipe cleaner into the shape of an antenna, and glue it to the head.
5. Have the child write one letter of his or her name on each of the other bottle caps with the marker.
6. Make a stand for the caterpillar by taking apart the clothespin and gluing the two halves end to end. It may be necessary to use more than one clothespin depending on the length of the child's name.
7. Starting with the caterpillar's head, begin gluing the caps, in order, to the clothespin.
8. Allow the caterpillar to dry thoroughly.

*C*hildren express themselves in a variety of ways, depending on their age, communication abilities, health status, and personality, to name just a few variables. Sensitively selected play opportunities can promote children's self-expression, an important adaptive technique for coping with stress. These activities also enable the health care professional to identify questions or concerns of the child. They can allow the child to develop coping techniques, while they serve as a vehicle for adults to respond to the child's communications. This chapter offers activities that can be used in these ways.

BACKGROUND INFORMATION

Current literature on coping has evolved from viewing it as a trait to seeing it as a process that varies with the situation and evolves over time (Folkman & Lazarus, 1980; Lazarus, 1980: Stone & Neale, 1984). Although individuals may respond in a similar manner to related situations, they do not necessarily respond the same way to new situations. Characteristics of the stress and coping process can vary, including the elicitors of coping behavior, the coping process itself, and the outcomes of coping.

Coping may be either action-focused or problem-focused (Lazarus & Folkman, 1984). Emotion-focused coping is used to regulate emotional responses to a problem, and problem-focused coping is directed toward taking specific steps to manage or change a difficult situation. Both types can be used in a given situation. Within each type of coping there are four coping modes: information-seeking, direct action, indirect action, and intrapsychic processes.

Children's coping is more complex since developmental changes over time affect children's abilities to appraise a stressor and identify coping resources available to them (Peterson, 1989). Caty, Ellerton, and Ritchie (1984) reviewed 39 published case studies of hospitalized children and analyzed the children's coping abilities using three dimensions of coping based on Lazarus's process model: information-exchange dimension, action/inaction dimension, and intrapsychic dimension. The information-exchange dimension included all verbal or nonverbal behavior involved in seeking, clarifying, confirming, or regulating information given or received. Caty et al categorized these behaviors into information-seeking behaviors, information-limiting behaviors, and information-giving behaviors. The action/inaction dimension included all noncognitive behaviors involved in managing self or environment by either taking action or pulling back. The subcategories in this dimension were mastery behaviors, controlling behaviors, tension-reducing behaviors, self-protective behaviors, self-comforting behaviors, behaviors soliciting assistance, behaviors expressing emotion, and behaviors indicating decision making toward independence or higher developmental level. The intrapsychic dimension consisted of the defense mechanisms, behaviors, and mental processes that regulate emotions and defend against anxiety: identification with another, projection, denial, displacement, regression, and intellectualization.

Subsequent research (Peterson, 1989) focuses on children's active, informative-seeking coping versus avoidant or information-denying coping. Other terms for these coping approaches are *sensitizer* and *repressor* coping styles (Field et al, 1988). Children who have avoidant or repressor styles respond less positively to the health care experience, according to research reviewed by Peterson (1989), as well as that conducted by Field et al (1988).

Descriptive research with hospitalized adolescents indicates that opportunities for self-expression via verbal, written, or other behavioral forms have been helpful, but not used much (cited in Denholm, 1990). Posthospital interviews with adolescents indicate that programming for adolescents contributed to more positive memories about the hospitalization experience as well as personal growth and insight gained from the experience. Interview research by Patton, Ventura, and Savedra (1986) reveals that ventilation of feelings was the fourth most often method of coping cited by adolescents with cystic fibrosis. Stevens (1989) interviewed adolescents before and after surgery and found that active coping, i.e., using physical or verbal activity at the time of the stressful encounter to try to alter it, was one technique identified by the youths.

Activities promoting self-expression can fall into several categories within the model defined by Caty and her colleagues. Mastery behaviors, behaviors expressing emotion, and behaviors indicating decision making toward independence or a higher developmental level can occur depending on the activity and child. The activities use emotion-focused as well as problem-focused coping.

Self-expression is also a component of active or information-seeking coping, which promotes more positive adjustment to health care experiences. The activities in this chapter can be used to promote this type of coping.

SPECIAL CONSIDERATIONS

Sufficient rapport should be established before doing self-expression activities with pediatric patients. Children and adolescents will be more likely to reveal thoughts and feelings to someone who is known and trusted. Activities should occur in a safe place, and patients should choose whether they wish to participate in the activity. The adult should be nonjudgmental and supportive.

Children and adolescents have different temperaments and communication styles that reflect individual differences. These preferences and styles should be considered when selecting a self-expression activity. For example, more indirect forms of communication are better for shyer, less open participants. The age of the child also determines the type of activity most appropriate, especially when it involves being able to identify feelings, write, or draw.

ACTIVITY GOALS

The activities in this chapter can be grouped according to three major goals based on how directly the child or adolescent is expressing feelings.

Indirect or Symbolic Communication

Some children may be reluctant or unable to communicate verbally. Activities like "Emotion Designs," "Feeling Faces," "Felt Puppets," and "Hospital Road Signs" are helpful with these children.

Identification and Discussion of Feelings

The next level of expression involves identifying and discussing feelings in more direct ways. "Pediatric Newspaper," "Things That Give Me A Lift," "Tongue Depressor Plaques," and "Feelings Game" can accomplish this goal.

Constructive Expression of Feelings

Children and adolescents may be ready to move beyond expression of feelings to coping with them. Activities like "Dear Doctor Letter," "Feelings Diary," "Graffiti Wall," and "Medical Play" can encourage pediatric patients to move to new and more advanced levels of coping.

Self-expression activities can provide an acceptable and safe outlet for anger, frustration, and aggression. Children do not always have the verbal skills to express feelings and thoughts. Often they do not have words to describe how they feel.

Once children have an acceptable means to express their emotions they are better equipped to handle stresses associated with hospitalization and illness.

ACTIVITY 7-1	*AUTOPHOTOGRAPHY*
Age Group	8 years through adolescence
Patient/Staff Ratio	1:1
Approximate Length	60 minutes
Therapeutic Rationale	To provide a vehicle for expression of feelings by: • Identifying objects that describe him or her • Photographing and writing about those objects • Displaying photographs in his or her room
Precautions and Restrictions	This activity requires the use of both hands. Check glue and marker precautions.
Required Skills	Participants must understand how to use a camera.
Equipment	Instant camera Film Flash cubes Cardboard Rubber cement Pen or marker
Implementation	1. Tell child that he or she will be taking 10 photographs that describe himself or herself. Some children may require a few examples to get them started. 2. After discussing the instructions, ask the child to compose a list of things he or she would like to photograph. 3. When the child is satisfied with the plan, supply a loaded camera with instructions to take photographs. 4. When all the photographs have been taken, have the child number them in order of importance or relevance. 5. Mount the photographs on cardboard using rubber cement. 6. Have the child write or dictate a description of the significance of each photograph. This may be inscribed beneath each picture. 7. With the child's permission, place the pictures in a prominent place where they may be viewed by staff, parents, and other patients.
Variation	Instead of mounting the photographs on cardboard, have the child place them in a hospital scrapbook.

<table>
<tr><td>

A C T I V I T Y   7 - 2

</td><td>

DEAR DOCTOR LETTER

</td></tr>
</table>

Age Group	8 years through adolescence
Patient/Staff Ratio	5:1
Approximate Length	20 minutes
Therapeutic Rationale	To provide a vehicle for expression of feelings by: • Identifying feelings about medical interventions • Writing about these feelings in a letter to the doctor
Precautions and Restrictions	This activity requires the use of both hands. Residents and attendants should be told about the activity and forth-coming letters.
Required Skills	Writing
Equipment	Paper Pencil Envelope
Implementation	1. Have the children write letters to their doctors expressing how they feel about medical intervention and the hospital. Encourage the children to express positive and negative feelings. 2. Assist the children with spelling or grammar upon request. 3. If the child desires, place the letters in the interoffice mail. Some children may be reluctant to send the letter because of fear of angering the doctor and subsequent repercussions. Such children may still enjoy the catharsis of writing their feelings and holding the letter to perhaps send at a later date.

ACTIVITY 7-5	*FEELING FACES*

Age Group 3 through 7 years

Patient/Staff Ratio 5:1

Approximate Length 15 minutes

Therapeutic Rationale To provide a vehicle for indirect or symbolic communication by:
- Creating a feeling face
- Using the feeling face to express

Precautions and Restrictions This activity requires the use of both hands.
Check marker and glue precautions.

Required Skills Pasting
Coloring

Equipment Tongue depressor
Marker
Paper plates
Paste

Implementation
1. Give each child two paper plates.
2. Have each child use markers to draw a happy face on one plate and a sad face on the other plate.
3. Paste the two faces back to back with a tongue depressor in the center. The child now has a flip-face, which shows a happy or sad face.
4. Discuss various emotional situations (e.g., parents leaving, getting a shot, or receiving a phone call from a friend).
5. Have the children use their "faces" to indicate how they would feel in these situations.
6. Allow the children to use the "faces" later during the hospital admission.

A C T I V I T Y 7 - 6

FEELINGS GAME

Age Group	4 through 8 years
Patient/Staff Ratio	5:1
Approximate Length	20 minutes
Therapeutic Rationale	To provide a vehicle for the identification and discussion of feelings by:

- Participating in feelings games
- Identifying situations in which he or she felt happy, sad, worried, angry, surprised, or frightened

Precautions and Restrictions   None

Required Skills   None

Equipment
Cardboard
Scissors
Markers
Dice
Ruler

Implementation

1. To make the game cut the cardboard into a circle, at least 1' in diameter.
2. Using a marker, divide the circle into six equal wedges.
3. In each segment draw a face depicting one of each of the following: happy, sad, worried, angry, surprised, and frightened.
4. To play the game, have children take turns throwing the die on the feelings wheel. Ask the children to describe a situation in which they had the same feeling as the face on the wheel where their die fell.
5. If the situation was negative for the child, have them tell how they coped with it. Assist the children in identifying more positive coping strategies when indicated.

A C T I V I T Y 7 - 7	*FELT PUPPETS*

Age Group

7 through 12 years

Patient/Staff Ratio

5:1

Approximate Length

30 to 45 minutes

Therapeutic Rationale

To provide a vehicle for indirect or symbolic communication by:
- Using the puppet to express feelings about the hospital
- Creating a story about the hospital

Precautions and Restrictions

This activity requires the use of both hands.
Check glue precautions.

Required Skills

Cutting
Pasting

Equipment

Felt
Puppet pattern (Fig. 7-2)
Felt scraps
Glue
Scissors

Implementation

1. Trace and cut out two puppet pieces for each child.
2. Give each child two precut puppet pieces.
3. Have the children put glue around the perimeter of one puppet piece, excluding the base where the child's hand will be inserted.
4. Press the two pieces together, matching the edges carefully.
5. Cut the features and clothing out of felt scraps and glue them in place.
6. Allow the puppet to dry completely.
7. Encourage the children to use the puppet to tell a story about the hospital. Ask open-ended questions that will promote the communication of the puppet's feelings, fears, and concerns about the hospital.

Felt Puppet

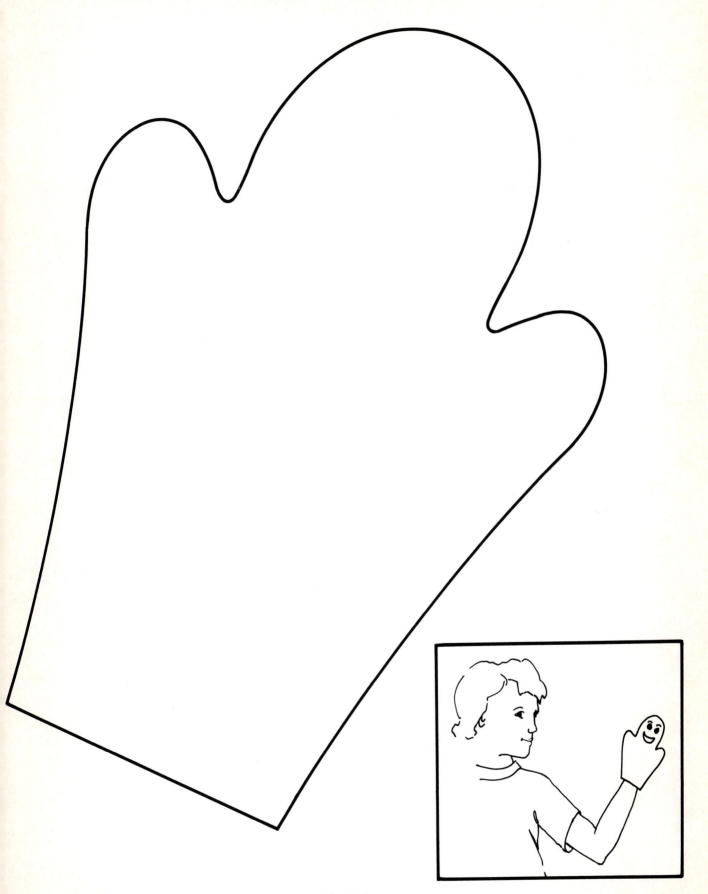

Fig. 7-2

ACTIVITY 7-8   *GRAFFITI WALL*

Age Group	10 years through adolescence
Patient/Staff Ratio	5:1
Approximate Length	Ongoing
Therapeutic Rationale	To provide a vehicle for expression of feelings by: • Using the graffiti wall to write positive and negative feelings about the hospital
Precautions and Restrictions	Children must have the use of one hand. Restrictions on the use of obscenities may be necessary. Check marker precautions.
Required Skills	Writing
Equipment	Large sheet of butcher paper or examining table paper Marker String Tape
Implementation	1. Tape the paper to a wall at a level that is within reach of the children. 2. Draw a vertical line dividing the paper in half. 3. Label one side with a positive statement, such as "Things I Like about the Hospital." 4. Label the other side with a negative statement, such as "Things I Dislike about the Hospital." 5. Tie one end of the string around the marker and tape the loose end to the wall next to the butcher paper. 6. Encourage all the children to contribute their feelings by writing them on the wall. 7. Allow for freedom of expression in an accepting, understanding atmosphere.

A C T I V I T Y 7 - 9	*HOSPITAL ROAD SIGNS*

Age Group	10 years through adolescence
Patient/Staff Ratio	5:1
Approximate Length	60 minutes
Therapeutic Rationale	To provide a vehicle for indirect or symbolic communication by: • Designing a road sign that expresses how they are feeling • Displaying a road sign as a way of communicating these feelings
Precautions and Restrictions	Children must have the use of both hands. Check marker precautions.
Required Skills	Cutting Coloring Drawing Writing
Equipment	Posterboard Scissors Markers Stencils (optional) Pictures of road signs (optional)
Implementation	1. Facilitate a discussion about how road signs communicate important information through the use of shapes, pictures, color, and words. Give examples: a triangle with the point down means "yield"; a red octagon means "stop"; a picture of a black truck encompassed by a red circle with a slash through it indicates "no trucks allowed." 2. Provide the children with posterboard, scissors, markers, and stencils. 3. Have the children create hospital road signs, using pictures, shapes, colors, and words to convey their messages. 4. If the children appear to need additional motivation, provide some suggestions. For example; a picture of a black syringe encompassed within a red circle with a red slash to indicate "no shots allowed."

ACTIVITY 7-10	*MEDICAL PLAY*

Age Group	2 years through adolescence
Patient/Staff Ratio	5:1
Approximate Length	45 minutes
Therapeutic Rationale	To provide a vehicle for expression of feelings by:
	• Acting out stressful medical procedures
	• Exploring hospital and medical implements
Precautions and Restrictions	Children should not be forced to participate in medical play.
	Children should be given freedom to play out experiences in their own way.
Required Skills	None
Equipment	Dolls
	Puppets
	Real medical equipment and supplies
	alcohol wipes
	tongue depressors
	tape
	swabs
	IV tubing
	stethoscopes
	blood pressure cuffs
	syringes without needles
	otoscopes
	surgical masks
	reflex hammers
	flashlights
	lab coats
	surgical gloves
	adhesive bandages
	Hospital play furniture
Implementation	1. If physical space is available, a medical play center should be established in the playroom. Medical play equipment should be readily available to the child when he or she expresses the need or desire to participate.
	2. Children should be allowed to play in their own way within necessary safety limitations.
	3. Be alert to children's misconceptions about the use of equipment and the possible need for additional time with a particular child.

ACTIVITY 7-11   *PEDIATRIC NEWSPAPER*

Age Group
7 years through adolescence

Patient/Staff Ratio
Not applicable

Approximate Length
Ongoing

Therapeutic Rationale
To provide a vehicle for the identification and discussion of feelings by:
  • Writing stories about the hospital for the pediatric newspaper

Precautions and Restrictions
Children who cannot write will need to dictate their story.

Required Skills
Reading
Writing

Equipment

Paper	Duplicating equipment
Pen	Stapler
Typewriter	

Implementation

1. Select a name and logo for the publication.
2. Establish a protocol for publication (e.g., length, how often it will be published, who will type it, how it will be duplicated).
3. Make a list of ideas or story starters for children who are difficult to motivate. Some possibilities are as follows:

editorials	interviews of hospital personnel
hospital crossword puzzle	jokes
hospital word search	opinion polls
hospital events	advice to the newly admitted

   Why I came to the hospital
   The nicest thing about my nurse
   Ten things that really scare me
   The first thing I want to do after I leave here is . . .
   If I were the head of this hospital, I would change . . .
4. When available, give the patients copies of old hospital newspapers.
5. Provide the children pen, paper, and encouragement. Allow them the freedom to write about whatever they wish. Avoid making writing a chore. Do not correct grammar or spelling since this may inhibit some children.
6. Obtain each contributor's home address, so that a copy of the newspaper can be mailed if they are discharged before the publication. A permanent mailing list may be compiled of children who are routinely hospitalized.
7. When sufficient material has been collected, duplicate the publication and staple it together.
8. Distribute the paper to staff members, administrators, and patients.

A C T I V I T Y   7 - 1 2

THINGS THAT GIVE ME A LIFT

Age Group	5 through 10 years
Patient/Staff Ratio	5:1
Approximate Length	30 minutes
Therapeutic Rationale	To provide a vehicle for the identification and discussion of feelings by:

- Discussing objects, people, and places that make the child feel good
- Writing down those things that make the child feel good.
- Displaying the poster in the child's room

Precautions and Restrictions

Participants must have the use of both hands.
Check marker and glue precautions.
Younger children will need to dictate their thoughts.

Required Skills

Cutting
Pasting
Tracing
Writing

Equipment

Balloon pattern (Fig. 7-3)
Construction paper
Markers
Scissors
Posterboard
Yarn
Glue

Implementation

1. Facilitate a discussion about pleasant events, people, or places that "give the children a lift." List all the things identified.
2. Instruct the children to trace the balloon shapes onto the construction paper and cut them out.
3. Have the children write one identified event, object, or place on each balloon.
4. Label the posterboard "Things That Give Me A Lift."
5. Have the children arrange the construction paper balloons on the posterboard, slightly overlapping, and glue them in place.
6. Make strings for the balloons with yarn and glue them in place.

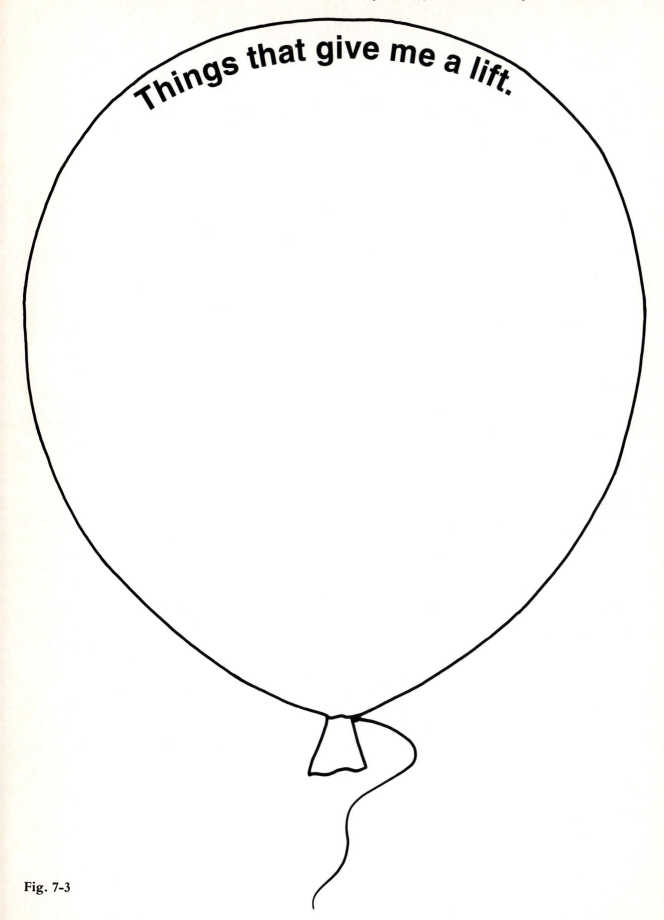

Fig. 7-3

ACTIVITY 7-13   *TONGUE DEPRESSOR PLAQUES*

Age Group	8 years through adolescence
Patient/Staff Ratio	5:1
Approximate Length	45 minutes
Therapeutic Rationale	To provide a vehicle for the identification and discussion of feelings by:

- Selecting a saying or statement that best describes his or her feelings
- Writing the statement on the tongue depressor plaque
- Displaying the plaque in his or her room

Precautions and Restrictions

Exercise discretion when using this activity within institutions having vermin problems.

Requires the use of both hands and good fine motor ability.

Check glue precautions.

Required Skills

Gluing

Equipment

Tongue depressors
Paint
Glue
Alphabet macaroni
Paint brush

Implementation

1. Help the child select a saying or statement he would like to use for his or her plaque, such as:
   "I Hate Shots"
   "Do Not Disturb"
   "Anne's Room"
2. Lay two tongue depressors vertically, 4 inches apart, to form the base (Fig. 7-4).
3. Glue additional tongue depressors side by side horizontally, across the base.
4. Allow the glue to dry completely.
5. The plaque may be painted at this point if desired.
6. Use the alphabet macaroni to spell out the desired message and glue on in place.

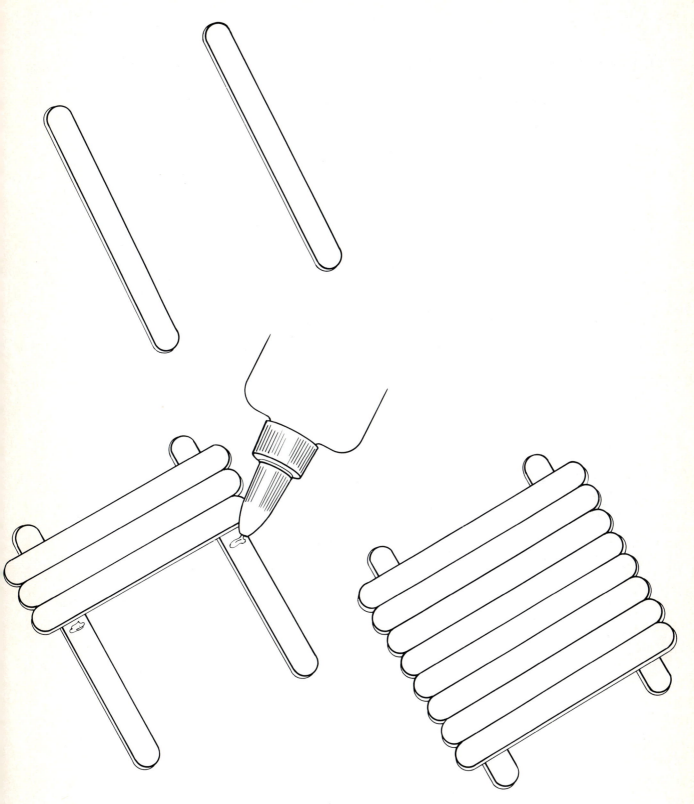

Fig. 7-4

ADDITIONAL IDEAS

- Use real or play telephones to promote verbalization during dramatic play.
- Use stories with appropriate themes to help children identify and discuss their feelings.
- Have children draw pictures of themselves in the hospital.
- Keep a suggestion box in the playroom.
- Encourage children to rewrite familiar songs using hospital themes.
- Have the children make protest signs to express their negative feelings.

REFERENCES

Caty, S., Ellerton, M.L. & Ritchie, J.A. (1984). Coping in hospitalized children: An analysis of published case studies. *Nursing Research, 33* (5), 277-282.

Denholm, G. (1990). Memories of adolescent hospitalization: Results from a 4-year follow-up study. *Children's Health Care, 19* (2), 101-105.

Field, T., Alpert, B., Vega-Lahr, M., Goldstein, S. & Perry, S. (1988). Hospitalization stress in children: Sensitizer and repressor coping styles. *Health Psychology, 7* (5), 433-445.

Folkman, S. & Lazarus, R.S. (1980). An analysis of coping in a middle-aged community sample. *Journal of Health and Social Behavior, 21,* 219-239.

Lazarus, R.S. (1980). The stress coping paradigm. In L.A. Bond & J.C. Rosen (Eds.), *Competence and coping during adulthood* (pp. 28-69). Hanover, NH: University Press of New England.

Patton, A.C., Ventura, J.N. & Savedra, M. (1986). Stress and coping responses of adolescents with cystic fibrosis. *Children's Health Care, 14* (3), 153-156.

Peterson, L. (1989). Coping by children undergoing stressful medical procedures: Some conceptual, methodological, and therapeutic issues. *Journal of Consulting & Clinical Psychology, 57* (3), 380-387.

Stevens, M. (1989). Coping strategies of hospitalized adolescents. *Children's Health Care, 18* (3), 163-169.

Stone, A.A. & Neale, J.M. (1984). New measures of daily coping: Development and preliminary results. *Journal of Personality & Social Psychology, 46,* 892-906.

CHAPTER 8

TENSION-RELEASE ACTIVITIES

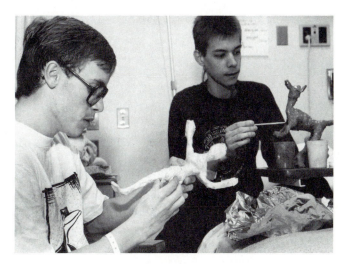

Fig. 8-1 Foil sculpture.

*P*lay is one of the most powerful and effective means of stress reduction for children. It is a natural activity that connotes normalization for the pediatric patient. Learning and adaptation can occur. Play can be a diversion for distancing from a stressful event. It can also be an outlet for expression of emotions and an opportunity for processing and dealing with stressful events. All of these aspects of play activities make them valuable tools for tension release. The activities in this chapter are designed to reduce tension by providing acceptable outlets for anger and aggression. Chapters with activities for self-expression and pain management supplement this chapter.

BACKGROUND INFORMATION

There is well documented evidence that children's common reactions to health care experiences include aggression, with physical aggression being more common among boys. The length of a hospital experience is associated with increased likelihood of aggression. Several studies also suggest that children who are more aggressive in the hospital tend to have better posthospital adjustment. (See review in Thompson, 1985.)

Current research focuses on describing the process people use when coping with the stresses of health care experience (see "self-expression," Chapter 7 introduction). Coping is now viewed as a process affected by many variables rather than a specific style used by the same person across all situations (Folkman & Lazarus, 1980; Lazarus, 1980; Stone & Neale, 1984). Children's coping is more complex since developmental changes over time affect children's abilities to appraise a stressor and identify coping resources available to them (Peterson, 1989).

Emotion-focused coping is used to regulate emotional responses to a problem, while problem-focused coping strategies are used to take directed steps to manage or change a difficult situation. One or both strategies can be used in a given situation. Within both of these coping strategies, there are four modes: information seeking, direct action, indirect action, and intrapsychic processes. Activities in this chapter involve action-focused coping, (Lazarus & Folkman, 1984).

Research by Ritchie, Caty, and Ellerton (1988) indicates that direct action is one of the most fre-

quently used coping responses for hospitalized preschoolers during both low-stress and high-stress events. This and other studies reveal that direct action behaviors for preschoolers include controlling, tension-reducing, and "attempting-to-protect-self-from-harm" behaviors. These behaviors reflect developmental concerns about autonomy and intrusion (Caty, Ellerton & Ritchie, 1984; Ellerton, Caty & Ritchie, 1985; Hyson, 1983; Ritchie, Caty & Ellerton, 1984).

School-aged children are able to identify stressful events and their reactions to them. In a study by Ryan (1989), elementary school and junior high school students listed coping strategies that were analyzed by type, sex, and ages of the children. Physical exercise and aggressive motor activities were identified as common coping strategies of the children. Boys cited physical exercise activities more often than girls. Analyses of case studies of hospitalized children reveals that sick children also use active methods to reduce tension (Caty, Ellerton & Ritchie, 1984). Interventions that allowed aggressive as well as other forms of play were therapeutic with school-aged children in a study by Clatworthy (1981).

Research with adolescents also indicates that this age group uses physical activity as a means for coping with hospitalization and chronic illness (Patton, Ventura & Savedra, 1986; Stevens, 1989). The amount of activity depended on illness limitations on this form of coping.

SPECIAL CONSIDERATIONS

Individual differences in strategies for coping will be reflected in the type of activity a child chooses. Aggressive tension-reducing activities are not for every patient. Other options may include activities in Chapters 7 and 13, dealing with self-expression or pain management.

Adults need to feel comfortable with noise and aggressive acts directed at the materials used in these activities. Often health care institutions are not responsive to such active means for children to express themselves; therefore, an appropriate location for these activities within a health care setting should be considered. Some activities involve messy play, so the setting should be appropriate also.

These activities allow for active physical

means for reducing tension rather than a problem-solving approach to work toward solutions. They offer outlets rather than solutions.

ACTIVITY GOALS

All of the activities in this chapter provide the means for safe and acceptable opportunities to express anger and frustration. "Aggression Cookies" and "Bread Dough Magnets" allow the children to work off tension and stress through an acceptable means: "Finger Painting" and "Punch Pillows" are activities that can assist the child to discuss causes of anger and begin to identify angry feelings. These activities also allow the child to regress in an acceptable way. This process in turn will promote physical release of tension. The activities involve various materials and all meet these same goals.

A C T I V I T Y 8 - 1	*AGGRESSION COOKIES*

Age Group	4 years through adolescence
Patient/Staff Ratio	5:1
Approximate Length	90 minutes
Therapeutic Rationale	To provide an acceptable safe outlet for anger, frustration, and aggression by: • Kneading, squeezing, and beating cookie dough
Precautions and Restrictions	Check the diets of all participants. Children must be closely supervised when using oven. Participants must wear gloves when handling food. Exercise discretion when using food in vermin-infested institutions.
Required Skills	None

Equipment	Surgical or examination gloves
	Oven
	Bowl
	Spoon
	Measuring cups and spoons
	Cookie sheet
	   3 cups flour
	   3 cups sugar
	   3 cups margarine
	   6 cups oatmeal
	   1 tablespoon baking soda
	   2 teaspoons vanilla extract

Implementation	1. Instruct the children to wash their hands and put on surgical or examination gloves. 2. Combine sugar, margarine, oatmeal, baking soda, vanilla extract, and flour in a bowl and mix lightly with a spoon. 3. Divide the dough into portions for each child. Instruct them to knead, squeeze, and beat the dough as much as they wish. 4. Form the dough into balls about the size of walnuts and place on an ungreased cookie sheet. 5. Bake at 350 degrees for 10 to 12 minutes. 6. Serve with milk and enjoy!

ACTIVITY 8-2

AGGRESSION PLAY WITH BLOCKS

Age Group	6 to 24 months
Patient/Staff Ratio	1:1
Approximate Length	10 minutes
Therapeutic Rationale	To provide an acceptable safe outlet for anger, frustration, and aggression by: • Building a block tower • Knocking over the block tower
Precautions and Restrictions	Avoid wooden and heavy blocks
Required Skills	Stacking
Equipment	6 to 10 cardboard, plastic, or other lightweight blocks
Implementation	1. Demonstrate how to build a tower, stacking the blocks on top of one another. 2. Knock the tower down. Show great pleasure in doing so. 3. Encourage the child to build a tower, assisting if necessary. 4. Urge the child to knock the tower down. Make sure the child is aware that this is acceptable and provide encouragement. 5. Repeat the activity until the child loses interest.

A C T I V I T Y 8 - 5	*BUBBLE PAINTING*

Age Group 3 through 10 years

Patient/Staff Ratio 5:1

Approximate Length 15 minutes

Therapeutic Rationale To promote physical release of tension by:
  • Using fingers and hands to paint with the bubble mixture

Precautions and Restrictions Children participating must have the use of one hand.

Required Skills None

Equipment
Large bowl
2 cups Ivory Flakes
1¾ to 2¼ cups water
Spoon
Eggbeater
Powdered tempera paint
Several emesis basins or other shallow containers
Cardboard

Implementation
1. Combine water with Ivory Flakes in a bowl.
2. Use the eggbeater to whip the mixture until stiff, adding more water if necessary.
3. Pour equal amounts of the mixture into the emesis basins.
4. Add tempera paint powder to each container, stirring with a spoon.
5. Have the children use their fingers to paint on the cardboard with the bubble paint.
6. Allow pictures to dry for 24 hours.

| A C | **A C T I V I T Y   8 - 6** | **CLASH, CLANG, AND CLATTER** |

Age Group	7 through 36 months
Patient/Staff Ratio	2:1
Approximate Length	10 minutes
Therapeutic Rationale	To promote physical release of tension by: • Making loud noises with toys and metal bowls
Precautions and Restrictions	All items used for this activity should be at least 3 inches in length and 1 inch in diameter.
Required Skills	Grasping Sitting
Equipment	Small, hard plastic objects Stainless steel bowl, at least 1 foot in diameter
Implementation	1. Drop a toy into the bowl causing the bowl to make a clanging noise. 2. Give the child a toy and encourage him or her to drop it into the bowl. 3. In an exaggerated manner, throw the toy into the bowl again and make a louder noise. 4. Encourage the child to mirror your actions. Clap when the child imitates your behavior. 5. Vary the activity by changing the position of the bowl and the toys used.

A C T I V I T Y 8 - 1 2   *SHOOTING GALLERY*

Age Group

3 through 10 years

Patient/Staff Ratio

5:1

Approximate Length

15 minutes (varies according to number of children playing)

Therapeutic Rationale

To provide an acceptable safe outlet for anger, frustration, and aggression by:

- Shooting the balls off the bottles

Precautions and Restrictions

Children must have the use of one hand.
Explicit limits should be set regarding where children may squirt water.
Children should be closely supervised.

Required Skills

None

Equipment

50 ml syringes, plastic spray bottles, basters, or squirt guns filled with water
Plastic bottles with small lid openings
Ping pong balls
Water
Masking tape

Implementation

1. Fill the bottles with enough water to weight them.
2. Place a ping pong ball on the top of each bottle, and line them up on a table.
3. Use the masking tape to create a line on the floor several feet back from the table.
4. Have the children stand at the designated line and use the syringes to squirt at the balls until they are knocked off the bottles.
5. Children may be divided into teams and the game can be played as a relay race.

A C T I V I T Y 8 - 1 3	*TARGET SQUIRTING*
Age Group	4 through 12 years
Patient/Staff Ratio	2:1
Approximate Length	20 minutes
Therapeutic Rationale	To provide an acceptable safe outlet for anger, frustration, and aggression by: • Squirting water at objects that cause stress to the child
Precautions and Restrictions	Explicit limitations should be placed on where the children may squirt water. Towels should be on hand to wipe water quickly off tile floors. Check marker precautions.
Required Skills	None
Equipment	Towels Posterboard Markers Clear contact paper Squirt guns or syringes without needles Water Basin
Implementation	1. On the posterboards draw representations of things that children do not like in the hospital. 2. Cover the poster with the contact paper and hang them on a wall over an uncarpeted floor. 3. Provide each children with a syringe or squirt gun. 4. Demonstrate how to fill the syringe or squirt gun with water and shoot at appropriate target. 5. Encourage children to squirt at the representations of things they don't like.

*T*he restrictions of immobilization and isolation place all patients at risk for both physical and psychological problems caused by loss of normal movement opportunities, sensory deprivation, and social isolation (Stewart, 1986). Pediatric patients are particularly at risk because physical interactions with a stimulating sensory and interpersonal environment are essential to their normal development (Karn & Ragiel, 1986). The activities in this chapter are designed to help prevent negative reactions and promote normal development in immobilized or isolated pediatric patients. Activities in Chapter 12 on perceptual-motor dysfunctions supplement the ones in this chapter.

BACKGROUND INFORMATION

Children who are immobilized or isolated feel a great sense of frustration because of their enforced confinement. Literature written before 1980 describes these feelings in case studies that also discuss children's coping mechanisms (see Akins, Mace & Akins, 1981). Recent studies of children's coping mechanisms reveal that variations in motor activity help children deal with stress (Caty, Ellerton & Ritchie, 1984), meaning that immobilized and isolated children may have fewer coping abilities available to them. Play can enable these children to express their feelings, and it allows the health care professional to identify as well as promote effective coping mechanisms (Ebmeier, 1982).

The pediatric patient's age also influences his reaction to immobilization and isolation (Ack, 1983; Karn & Ragiel, 1986; Kidder, 1989). In children less than 6 months old, there is less observable reaction to immobilization. Professionals believe that the young infant is unable to distinguish immobilization from normal life and quickly adapts *as long as* his or her physical and emotional needs are met. From 6 to 18 months, separation anxiety is a major factor influencing the child's reactions to immobilization and isolation, with children becoming visibly upset when parents and significant others leave the room or bedside. Toddlers have difficulty understanding the reason for their restraint or isolation, resulting in regression and restlessness. Preschoolers experience guilt and explore their environment less under these conditions. The school-aged child's greatest fear is loss of control. Anger and hostility result when the

child is physically or socially restrained. Initial feelings of frustration in school-aged, immobilized patients dissipate as they assume one of several roles to deal with the situation. The selected role is usually a variation of one of three behavioral patterns: responsibly independent, passively dependent, or manipulative (Swanson, 1980). The adolescent is most concerned about body image and fear of being different from peers. Adolescents are also developing their independence from family, so depression and frustration can occur because of the adolescent's increased dependency. Acting out, regression, anger, denial, and hostility are all reactions to physical and social restraints. As health improves, boredom and apathy are possible problems (Ack, 1983; Karn & Ragiel, 1986; Kidder, 1989).

Regardless of the pediatric patient's age, he or she is at risk when immobilized or isolated due to restrictions in movement, space, and contact with the environment. Orientation to time and place is affected. Loss of bodily and environmental control are also major challenges. Reduced interactions with the environment and the people in it can result in depersonalization. All of these factors threaten the child's self-image and self-esteem. Fortunately, there is documented evidence that play activities are helpful in overcoming the potentially harmful effects from these aspects of immobility and isolation (Gillis, 1989; Gottlieb & Portnoy, 1988; Linn, Beardslee & Patenaude, 1986; O'Connell, 1984; Pfander & Bradley-Johnson, 1990; Tarnow & Gutstein, 1983).

SPECIAL CONSIDERATIONS

Karn and Ragiel (1986) emphasize the importance of assessing a child for the effects of immobilization; this would also be true for isolated children. They recommend the following nine areas for assessment:

1. Age-appropriate behaviors and capacities
2. Support system
3. School performance
4. Content of play
5. Thought processes
6. Dietary and elimination patterns
7. Medication use
8. Activity level
9. Sleep patterns

Evaluating these nine areas can provide information about the specific concerns of the child and his or her level of adjustment. It can indicate needed play interventions and reveal appropriate play activities.

ACTIVITY GOALS

The activities in this chapter are grouped into five purposes: providing sensory stimulation, stimulating kinesthesia, promoting orientation to time and place, encouraging social interactions, and reducing depersonalization. Some activities have dual purposes.

Sensory Stimulation

Sensory stimulation involves providing activities that stimulate the five senses. Activities such as "Kool-Aid Play Dough," "Cooking/Baking," "Pudding Paint," and "Finger Painting", Chapter 8, can achieve this goal.

Kinesthesia

Kinesthesia, or a sense of movement, can be real or perceived. Perceived or real movement beyond the area of confinement is particularly helpful for children who are immobilized or isolated. Real movement experiences are provided in

"Fishing Game" and "Basketball." Perceived movement can be achieved via "Special Place Collages." To simulate movement beyond the area of confinement, activities such as, "Using Remote Control Car," "Flashlight Play," "Fishing Game," and "Traction Basketball" can be used.

Orientation to Time and Place

Activities that help the child remain oriented to current time and place are especially helpful during prolonged immobilization or isolation. "Unit Scrapbook," as well as a calendar and a daily schedule, can accomplish this goal.

Social Interactions

Interventions that reduce social isolation, such as "Isolation Pen Pals" and "Walkie Talkie," are important for restricted pediatric patients.

Reducing Depersonalization

Children need to maintain a sense of self and their relationship to others outside the hospital. Bringing in family photos, toys, a pillow or bedspread from home, and a favorite home-cooked meal can accomplish this goal. These ideas and others are listed in the Additional Ideas section of this chapter.

A C T I V I T Y 1 0 - 1	*AROMA JARS*

Age Group	3 through 7 years
Patient/Staff Ratio	3:1
Approximate Length	10 minutes
Therapeutic Rationale	To increase appetite by: • Smelling foods with strong odors
Precautions and Restrictions	Do not use substances that may evoke an allergic reaction.
Required Skills	None

Equipment	Specimen cups with screw-on lids or baby food jars
	Any food with a distinct, appetizing odor such as:
	    Cinnamon
	    Cocoa mix
	    Drink mix
	    Lemon peel
	    Peppermint
	    Ripe banana
	    Strawberry

Implementation	1. Place one ingredient in each cup or jar. 2. Ask the children to close their eyes and smell each cup. Encourage them to inhale deeply. 3. Ask each child to identify the odor. Make the activity into a game by having children close their eyes when smelling. 4. Have the children taste the food to see if they are correct.
Variation	Use scratch and sniff stickers with appealing food scents.

A C T I V I T Y 1 0 - 2	*AWARD CERTIFICATES*

Age Group	3 to 10 years
Patient/Staff Ratio	1:1
Approximate Length	Ongoing activity
Therapeutic Rationale	To improve patient cooperation by: • Performing the desired behavior to receive a reward certificate
Precautions and Restrictions	Awards must be given for specific predetermined behaviors. Parents and staff members must support an award program and help determine which behaviors will be rewarded. Children must see the award certificate as a valuable item and be willing to work to receive one.
Required Skills	None
Equipment	Award certificates (Fig. 10-2) Pen or marker
Implementation	1. Award certificates should be filled out and given at the time the child displays positive behaviors or coping mechanisms. 2. Appropriate behaviors to award include: Holding still for shots or drawing blood Taking medicine Fnishing a meal Participating in care Using call light appropriately Drinking extra fluids Cooperating with difficult therapy regimen 3. Personalize the award by filling in the child's name and the behavior to which you are paying tribute. 4. Encourage the child to select a prominent place to display the award, and have staff members and parents praise the child for the achievement.

Daily Weight Record

Name:_____   Doctor:_____

Date:_____	Date:_____	Date:_____
Date:_____	Date:_____	Date:_____
Date:_____	Date:_____	Date:_____
Date:_____	Date:_____	Date:_____
Date:_____	Date:_____	Date:_____
Date:_____	Date:_____	Date:_____

Fig. 10-3

A C T I V I T Y 1 0 - 6	*FOOT PAINTING*

Age Group	3 through 10 years
Patient/Staff Ratio	3:1
Approximate Length	30 minutes
Therapeutic Rationale	To encourage ambulation and provide exercise by: • Making a foot painting
Precautions and Restrictions	Floor play area should be a safe surface.
Required Skills	None
Equipment	Large basins filled with 2 inches of water Roll of butcher paper Tempera paint Towels Soap Wash basin filled with soapy water Music
Implementation	1. Add enough tempera paint to one basin to color the water. 2. Have all the participants wash their feet. 3. Place one 8-foot long sheet of butcher paper on the floor for each child. 4. Have each child place his or her feet in a basin of paint. 5. Instruct the children to create designs on the butcher paper by walking on it.
Variation	Encourage the children to dance to music and paint simultaneously.

ACTIVITY 10-7   *FOOT PUPPETS*

Age Group	5 through 12 years
Patient/Staff Ratio	1:1
Approximate Length	30 minutes

Therapeutic Rationale

To increase blood circulation and movement of the legs by:
- Participating in a foot puppet show

Precautions and Restrictions

The child must have the use of both hands.
Check glue and scissors precautions.
Use disposable needles instead of reusing needles. Follow the institution's guidelines for the disposal of sharp objects. Usually specific containers are indicated.

Required Skills

Cutting
Pasting

Equipment

Old socks
Scrap materials (e.g., cloth, buttons, yarn)
Glue
Needle and thread
Scissors

Implementation

1. Have the child select a theme for his or her puppet show, using two characters.
2. Have the child make two puppets by cutting the features out of scrap materials and either sewing or gluing them in place on the sock.
3. Yarn may be used to make the puppets' hair.
4. The method used to perform with the foot puppets will depend on limitations imposed by the child's condition. If the child is on bed rest, dangling the legs over the end of the bed or resting them on top of a bedside table is a possibility.
5. Encourage the child to incorporate movement into his or her performance.
6. If possible, provide a mirror so that the child may view his or her own puppet show.

A C T I V I T Y 1 0 - 8   *GROUP MEALS*

Age Group	3 years through adolescence
Patient/Staff Ratio	5:1
Approximate Length	45 minutes
Therapeutic Rationale	To normalize meals and encourage food intake by:
	• Participating in group meals
Precautions and Restrictions	A volunteer or staff member must be present to supervise, assist, and observe children.
	Children on restricted diets must be assessed to determine if observing others eating normally will upset them.
Required Skills	None

Equipment

Tablecloth or sheet	Napkins
Table large enough to seat participants comfortably	Food
	Index cards
Eating utensils	Markers

Implementation

1. Make a place card for each patient by writing the child's name on the bottom of an index card and folding it in half to make it stand.
2. Cover the table with a sheet or tablecloth.
3. When the meal trays are delivered, remove the child's food and utensils and arrange them at his or her place on the table. Check the trays to be sure that all foods ordered have been provided appropriately.
4. Have the children wash their hands, take their seat, and begin eating.
5. Engage the children in conversation about their favorite foods, good nutrition, and other related topics.
6. Praise the children when they display desired eating habits.
7. Have the children participate in cleanup activities.
8. Make note of what each child consumed and report this if necessary.
9. Parents and siblings should be included in meals whenever possible.

Variations

Ambulatory adolescents may enjoy a group dinner in the cafeteria. This would require special arrangements with nursing, dietary, as well as administrative approval.

If no dietary restrictions exist, meals may be served family style, allowing the children to select the food and portions they desire.

Toddlers also benefit from dining in group situations. Be sure to place highchairs far enough apart so that toddlers cannot reach each other.

REFERENCES

Azarnoff, P. & Woody, P.D. (1981). Preparation of children for hospitalization in acute care hospitals in the United States. *Pediatrics, 68* (3), 361-368.

Broome, M. & Hellier, A. (1987). Schoolage children's fears of medical experiences. *Issues in Comprehensive Pedriatric Nursing, 10,* 77—86.

Denholm, C.J. (1985). Hospitalization and the adolescent patient: A review and some critical questions. *Child Health Care, 14* (2), 109-116.

Denholm, C.J. & Ferguson, R.V. (1987). Strategies to promote the developmental needs of hospitalized adolescents. *Child Health Care, 15* (3), 183-187.

Epstein, L.H., Wing, R.R., & Valoski, A. (1985). Childhood obesity. *Pediatric Clinics of North America, 32* (2), 363-379.

Fosson, A. & deQuan, M.M. (1984). Reassuring and talking with hospitalized children. *Child Health Care, 13* (1), 37-44.

Foster, R.L., Hunsberger, M.M., & Anderson, J.J. (1989). *Family Centered Nursing Care of Children.* Philadelphia: W.B. Saunders Company.

Groer, M.W. (1981). *Physiology and pathophysiology of the body fluids.* St. Louis: The CV Mosby Co.

Guyton, A.D. (1982). *Human physiology and mechanisms of disease* (3rd ed.). W.B. Saunders.

Hedberg, A.M., Garcia, J., & Weinmann-Wenkler, M. (1988). Nutritional risk screening: Development of a standardized protocol. *Journal of the American Dietetic Association, 88* (2), 1553-1556.

Joos, S.K., & Pollett, E. (1987). Nutritional status and behavior. In R. Grand, J. Sutphen, & W. Deitz (Eds.), *Pediatric Nutrition: Theory and Practice.* Butterworth Publishers.

Karn, M.A. & Ragiel, C.A. (1986). The psychologic effects of immobilization on the pediatric patient. *Orthopaedic Nursing, 5* (6), 12-17.

Keane, S., Garralda, M.E., & Keen, J.H. (1986). Resident parents during pediatric admissions. *International Journal of Nursing Studies, 23* (3), 247-253.

LaMontagne, L.L. (1984). Children's locus of control beliefs as predictors of preoperative behavior. *Nursing Research, 33,* 76-79.

Lowrey, G. (1986). *Growth and development of children* (8th ed.). Chicago: Year Book Medical Publishers.

Lucas, B., Rees, J.M., & Mahan, L.K. (1989). *Nutrition in childhood* (8th ed.). Philadelphia: W.B. Saunders, Co.

Miller, S.A. (1987). Promoting self-esteem in the hospitalized adolescent: Clinical interventions. *Issues Comprehensive Pediatric Nursing, 10,* 187-194.

Pass, M.D. & Pass, E.M. (1987). Anticipatory guidance for parents of hospitalized children. *Journal of Pediatric Nursing, 2* (4), 250-258.

Petrillo, M. & Sanger, S. (1980). *Emotional care of hospitalized children* (2nd ed.). Philadelphia: J.B. Lippincott Co.

Pipes, P.L. (1989). *Nutrition in infancy and childhood* (4th ed.). St. Louis: Mosby–Year Book, Inc.

Robinson, C.A. (1986). Preschool children's conceptualizations of health and illness. *Child Health Care, 16* (2), 89-95.

Scipien, G., Barnard, M., Chard, M., Howe, J., & Phillips, P. (1986). *Comprehensive pediatric nursing,* New York: Mc-Graw-Hill.

Sperhac, A.M. (1990). Nutritional assessment. In S.R. Mott, S.R. James, & A.M. Sperhac (Eds.), *Nursing care of children.* California: Addison-Wesley.

Terry, D.G. (1987). The needs of parents of hospitalized children. *Child Health Care, 16* (1), 18-20.

Thompson, R.H. (1985). Psychosocial research on pediatric hospitalization and health care: A review of the literature, Springfield, Il: Charles C Thomas, Publisher.

Waechter, E., Phillips, J. & Holladay, B. (1985). *Nursing Care of Children* (10th ed.). Philadelphia: J.B. Lippincott.

Walker, W.A. & Hendrichs, K.M. (1985). *Manual of pediatric nutrition,* W.B. Saunders, Co.

Whaley, L. & Wong, D. (1991). *Nursing care of infants and children.* (4th ed.). St. Louis: Mosby–Year Book, Inc.

CHAPTER 11

BREATHING GAMES

Fig. 11-1 Maze.

Activities   11-1   Balloon Football
                11-2   Balloon Rockets
                11-3   Bubble Printing
                11-4   Cottonball Hockey
                11-5   Kazoos
                11-6   Maze
                11-7   Pinwheels
                11-8   Sailboat Blowing
                11-9   Straw Blow Painting
                11-10   Tuned Bottle Blowing

Some of the most common health problems in the pediatric age group are related to disturbed respiratory function, with respiratory failure as the chief cause of morbidity in the newborn period (Kendig & Chernick, 1983). Respiratory problems in children can be caused by disease, trauma, and physical anomalies or can be seen as a manifestation of a disturbance in another organ or system. Most communicable diseases have respiratory system involvement (Whaley & Wong, 1991).

Health care providers designing play activities for pediatric patients with diminished lung expansion, impaired air flow, or other abnormalities that interfere with respiratory function must understand that developmental differences exist between the child and adult respiratory systems. The size and position of a child's airway allows it to be easily obstructed with any respiratory disease. Even a minimal amount of swelling and inflammation along the airway can create respiratory distress in a child (Whaley & Wong, 1991; Feeg & Harbin, 1991). Airways of the infant and young child are less developed than in the adult; therefore, they are more easily obstructed by nausea, blood, or edema (Behrman & Vaughn, 1987; Blazer, Navek & Friedman, 1980; Hagedown, Gardner, & Abman, 1989). In the young infant the ribs are more pliable and fail to support the lungs, leading to retractions with respiratory problems. Respirations are further compromised when the chest cannot compensate, as in the child with asthma or abdominal distention (Ellis, 1988).

A child has a higher metabolic rate in comparison to an adult; therefore, a pulmonary illness that compromises respiratory function can result in increased metabolic demands and oxygen consumption. For example, in a child with bronchiolitis, the illness may interfere with air exchange in the lungs (Wohl, 1986). For any child with respiratory problems, having information about the child's present illness is important (e.g., Is this an acute illness? Does the child have recurrent upper or lower respiratory tract infections?).

Some diseases of the lungs, such as cystic fibrosis, are inherited. Diseases, such as asthma or bronchitis, have both genetic and environmental causes. It is not uncommon to find that irritants in the environment may exacerbate asthmatic symptoms. Pets, vegetation, color dyes, toys, and secondary smoke can be possible irritants (Bronniman & Burrows, 1986).

Coughing is a protective reflex of the respiratory system. The child with asthma or cystic fibrosis typically coughs more in the early morning and upon awakening (Ellis, 1988). A child with a respiratory infection is more likely to have a loose-sounding, productive cough rather than a dry, nonproductive cough.

BACKGROUND INFORMATION

Young children are unable to describe difficulty breathing (dyspnea); however, one can look for clues in observing the child's behavior during activity. The child may exhibit decreased exercise tolerance or shortness of breath with activity. A child having some shortness of breath may be quiet, inactive, or lack interest and enthusiasm for play activities. Children with pulmonary edema or asthma may be uncomfortable except in a semi-sitting position. The child may prop himself up and rest his weight on his arms. Children with asthma and cystic fibrosis frequently have retractions when they breathe. Grunting and nasal flaring are most frequently seen in young children in respiratory distress.

The child with chronic respiratory disease may have repeated hospital admissions for a variety of reasons. These children often require numerous medications and therapies to control respiratory symptoms (Carroll, 1987). Understanding the action and side effects of the medications and daily treatments is essential for an individual working with children who have chronic respiratory problems. Some of the treatments, such as chest physiotherapy, are time consuming, whereas other treatments are expensive and unpleasant for the child. Any of these inconveniences may foster stress and anxiety in both the child and family.

Children with respiratory disease may require an additional source of oxygen both in the hospital and at home. A nasal cannula is the most common method for administering the oxygen. The nasal cannula can be irritating because it is usually held in place by tape applied to the face. If one is caring for a child requiring supplemental oxygen, understanding how to change and secure the cannula may be necessary.

Children with respiratory problems, whether acute or chronic, have altered nutritional requirements. Most children experiencing respiratory dysfunction have difficulty eating during acute episodes. Unfortunately, it is at this time that it is usually necessary for the child to at least maintain or even increase caloric intake (Clough, Lindenauer, Hayes, & Zekany, 1986). Children with respiratory problems also require favorite fluids at frequent intervals. Adequate hydration is essential for any child with an illness that causes mucus production in order to keep the mucus from becoming thick and tenacious (Zahr, Connolly, & Page, 1989).

During the acute phase of a respiratory disease process, a child may suffer sleep deprivation. Frequent coughing, which is most prevalent at night, may interrupt the child's sleep pattern; therefore, a child may require quiet times during the day to rest. Activities may need to be planned that conserve the child's energy.

The child with respiratory dysfunction may have pain from bronchospasms or as the result of injections for therapy. Each child's pain experience is unique. For further information about assessment and management of pediatric pain, refer to Chapter 13. Distraction and other pain relief measures are also discussed.

Children with chronic respiratory problems have physical changes. For example, the child with cystic fibrosis may experience a barrel chest, pallor, short stature, and clubbing of fingernails and toenails. The child may view his body as inferior because of the physical limitations. The child who has to take breaks to rest or cough may be teased or not asked to participate in normal activities. The child may be avoided by peers who do not understand chronic respiratory problems. Strategies to help the child cope with difficult situations are an important part of the overall management for respiratory problems. Role playing, as well as support groups, can be helpful (Meyers, 1988; Romero, 1986).

Children with respiratory dysfunction need to continue their normal developmental progress, like other hospitalized children. To promote growth and development, diversional activities should be provided that are appropriate to age, play ability, interest, and peer involvement. The

activity may need to be started slowly and the tempo gradually increased as tolerance improves. The ideal selected activity may be one at which the child can define the pace. Peer activity is important because social skills of communication, interaction, and sharing can only be learned in a social situation (Kaluger & Kaluger, 1984; LaMontagne, 1984; Shaffer, 1985).

Effectively designed play activities should be an integral part of a treatment plan for pediatric patients with respiratory dysfunction. Play activities can provide the child with an incentive to comply with numerous medical treatments. Children benefit psychologically from activities that help to relieve the stress and anxiety associated with an illness and provide the child with a sense of control.

Care must be taken that appropriate activities are used with respiratory patients. It is important to consult the physician caring for the child to discuss any restrictions before beginning activities.

SPECIAL CONSIDERATIONS
Surgical Patients

The intensity of therapeutic activities with surgical patients depends on the type of surgery, the location and size of incision, and the amount of mobility allowed during the recuperative process. Following any use of general anesthesia, respiratory exercises that promote alveolar expansion and exchange of oxygen and carbon dioxide are usually encouraged. The child, however, may be reluctant to do such exercises because of the fear of pain and concern about "opening" the surgical incision. The child will need reassurance that the incision is secure. The use of a pillow or supportive hands over the incision site often lessens the fear of the wound opening. Following certain neurologic and ophthalmologic surgery, coughing may be contraindicated. Be sure to check for restrictions before involving the child in any activities.

The Child with Tracheostomy

Some children require an artificial airway (tracheostomy tube) for long-term ventilation. Such a tube can be secured in place and the child can be allowed to participate in activities as tolerated.

Today many children are discharged from hospitals with a tracheostomy and cared for at home. In planning activities for a child with a tracheostomy, the following should be considered:

1. Monitor the child's play so fingers, food, or toys are not put into the tracheostomy tube. Make sure the tube does not inadvertently come out during activities.
2. Do not use stuffed toys or fine-haired pets that shed because hair and lint can obstruct the trachea.
3. Supervise the child during any water play activities.
4. Do not use activities involving powders or aerosol sprays.
5. Have a portable suction machine and catheter available in the recreation area in case the tracheostomy tube becomes obstructed. If no clinical staff members are available, the individual providing diversional activities must be instructed on the proper management of the child with a tracheostomy.

Most of the activities in this chapter require mild-to-moderate expenditure of energy. Children with cardiac or respiratory conditions should be monitored for any sign of difficult breathing or shortness of breath with exertion. If the child's breathing changes, he seems "out of breath," or his activity level decreases, the activity should be discontinued. The child should be assisted to a resting position and evaluated by a physician.

ACTIVITY GOALS AND INFORMATION

Since activities in this book involve the use of balloons, a few words of caution are necessary. Balloons should not be used with children under 3 years or with any child who developmentally cannot follow directions because of the risk of aspiration. Activities that involve repetitive balloon inflation require deep breaths and the use of respiratory muscles. Be sure to use balloons that are pliable.

The activities in this chapter can be grouped according to the major goals of promoting coughing, deep breathing, and pursed-lip breathing.

Promoting Coughing

Coughing can be encouraged by having the child huff or exhale several breaths with successively increasing rapidity and force. The child frequently feels and acts on the urge to cough without ever being told to do so (Cosenza & Celentano, 1986; Whaley & Wong, 1991). Activities such as "Balloon Rockets," "Cottonball Hockey," and "Sailboat Blowing" foster the use of breathing during play.

Promoting Deep Breathing

Activities to promote deep breathing require slow, deep inhalation for best effect. This type of breathing promotes full expansion of the alveoli in all lobes of the lungs. The use of incentive inspirometers rewards the patient for deep inhalation and de-emphasizes the exhalation phase of respiration (Cosenza & Celentano, 1986). Activities such as "Aroma Jars" and "Kazoos" require moderate-to-deep breaths to implement them. Be sure the child does not have any allergies associated with the respiratory dysfunction.

Promoting Pursed-Lip Breathing

Asthmatic children are often taught to use a pursed-lip breathing technique to help open and maintain a clear airway. To perform pursed-lip breathing the child takes a slow, deep breath. During the slow exhalation through the mouth, the lips are pursed or puckered. This increases the air resistance during the exhalation phase. This breathing method maintains some positive end-expiratory pressure within the alveoli preventing complete collapse of these elastic air sacs and prolonging the air exchange portion of the respiratory sequence (Tiep et al, 1986). "Pinwheels," "Bubble Printing," "Straw Blow Painting," "Tuned Bottle Blowing," and blowing pieces of paper with a straw along a tabletop race track are activities that can encourage a child to use pursed-lip breathing techniques.

A C T I V I T Y   1 1 - 1

BALLOON FOOTBALL

Age Group	5 through 8 years
Patient/Staff Ratio	4:1
Approximate Length	30 minutes
Therapeutic Rationale	To promote: • Lung expansion • Increasing expiratory volume • Clearing airways of mucus and secretions
Precautions and Restrictions	Balloons should be used with caution and collected at the end of each activity session. Infants and toddlers should not be given balloons. Check balloon precautions.
Required Skills	None
Equipment	Balloon Table
Implementation	1. This game is played with an even number of players divided into two teams. 2. The teams line up on opposite sides of the table. 3. An inflated balloon is placed in the center of the table. Each team tries to blow the balloon off the opposing team's side of the table. 4. The players may not touch the balloon with any part of their body. 5. The first team to make five goals wins.

ACTIVITY 11-2	*BALLOON ROCKETS*

Age Group 5 through 12

Patient/Staff Ratio 5:1

Approximate Length 30 minutes

Therapeutic Rationale To promote:
- Lung expansion
- Deep breathing

Precautions and Restrictions This activity is not appropriate for patients with asthma.
Check balloon precautions.
Check scissor precautions.

Required Skills Cutting

Equipment Long balloon
Rubber band
Plastic straw
Construction paper
Scissors

Implementation
1. Instruct the children to cut the straw in half (Fig. 11-2).
2. Have them fold the tip of one of the straw halves so it will insert into the other half.
3. Push the straw half until it is completely inside the other straw.
4. Tell the children to insert the straw into the neck of the balloon and secure tightly in place with a rubber band.
5. Have the children cut the construction paper into a 4-inch square and fold it in half.
6. Have them make a small hole in the center of the fold and push the straw through it. The balloon, straw, and construction paper make the rocket.
7. To launch the rocket, blow the balloon up through the straw and let it go. The rocket direction can be adjusted by changing the shape and size of the construction paper. The rocket's speed may be regulated by closing or opening the straw vent.

Steps 1-3

Step 4

Step 5

Step 6

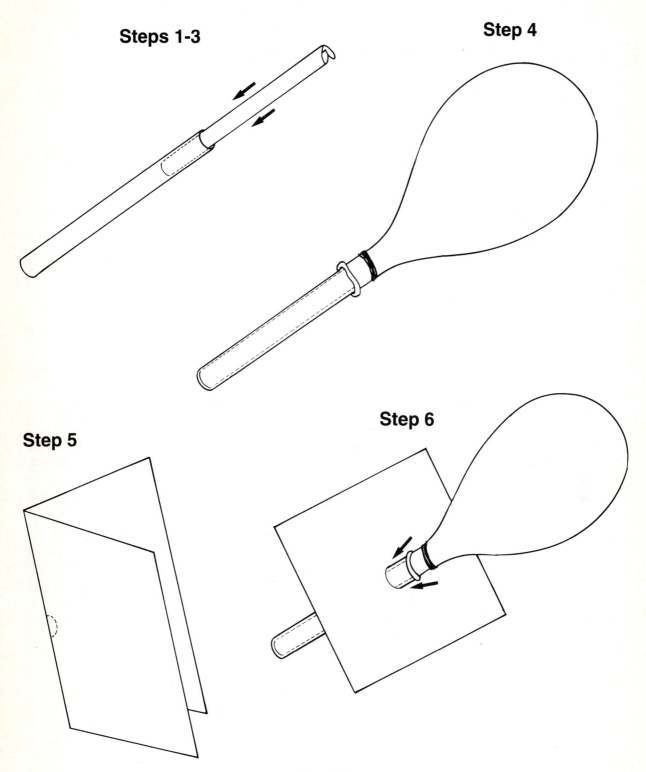

Fig. 11-2

A C T I V I T Y 1 1 - 3	***BUBBLE PRINTING***

Age Group	5 through 12 years
Patient/Staff Ratio	5:1
Approximate Length	20 minutes
Therapeutic Rationale	To promote: • Lung expansion • Clearing airways of mucus and secretions
Precautions and Restrictions	Children participating must have the use of one hand. Children need to be carefully supervised so that they do not aspirate or ingest the paint. Let the children practice first using a mixture of water and food coloring. Check the child's tongue for coloring to ensure that the activity is being correctly done.
Required Skills	Blowing
Equipment	Liquid soap detergent Liquid tempera paint Straw or 4-inch piece of IV tubing Paper Emesis basins or shallow containers Water
Implementation	1. To prepare the bubble mixture, combine one part tempera paint with one part detergent in an emesis basin. Add about 1 cup of water to the mixture. 2. Tell the children to place one end of a straw in the paint mixture and blow through the other end. Make sure the children blow through the straw and do not accidently suck the mixture into their mouths. 3. When the soap bubbles rise above the edge of the container, have the child hold a piece of paper horizontally above the bubbles. 4. Slowly lower the paper until it touches the bubbles. 5. Repeat the process with several colors.

ACTIVITY 11-4

COTTONBALL HOCKEY

Age Group 6 through 13 years

Patient/Staff Ratio 2:1

Approximate Length 20 minutes

Therapeutic Rationale To promote:
- Lung expansion
- Deep breathing

Precautions and Restrictions Children participating must have the use of one hand.

Required Skills None

Equipment Cardboard box lid 18″ × 24″
Plastic margarine tubs (2)
Scissors
Glue
Cottonball
Straws (2)

Implementation
1. Place the box, rim side up, in front of you.
2. Cut a 2-inch section out of each margarine tub (Fig. 11-3).
3. Glue one margarine tub to each end of the box top. The cut out section of the margarine tub should face the center of the long box. These form the "goal."
4. Place a cottonball in the center of the box.
5. Give each child a straw and have them try to blow the cotton ball into the opponent's goal.

Margarine tub

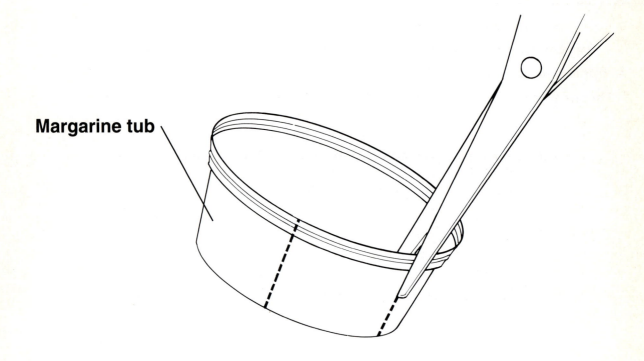

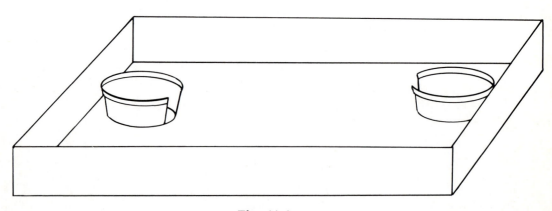

Fig. 11-3

A C T I V I T Y 1 1 - 5	*KAZOOS*
Age Group	3 through 8 years
Patient/Staff Ratio	5:1
Approximate Length	30 minutes
Therapeutic Rationale	To promote: • Lung expansion • Deep breathing
Precautions and Restrictions	Children participating in this activity must have the use of both hands. Young children will require assistance puncturing the tube. Check scissors precautions.
Required Skills	Cutting
Equipment	Cardboard tube Paint Brush Rubber band Wax paper Scissors or other sharp instrument
Implementation	1. Have the children paint the tube, leaving a 1-inch space at one end unpainted (Fig. 11-4). 2. When the paint has dried, the activity leader should use a sharp instrument to put three holes 2 inches apart vertically along the tube. 3. Cut a circle of wax paper 1 inch larger than the diameter of the tube. 4. Have the children mold the wax paper to cover the opening of the painted end of the tube and secure it with a rubber band. 5. Have the children sing, whistle, or hum into the open end of the kazoo.
Variation	Commercially manufactured kazoos may also be used.

KAZOO

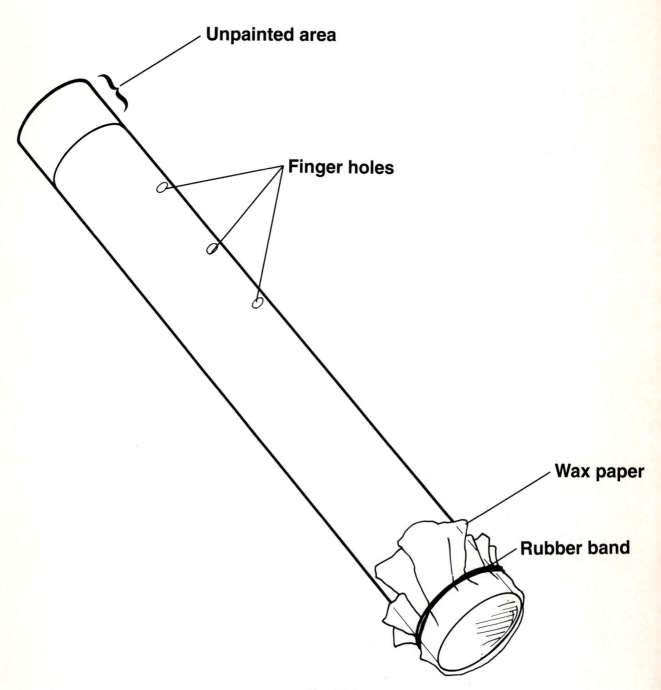

Fig. 11-4

A C T I V I T Y 1 1 - 6	*MAZE*

Age Group	4 through 12 years
Patient/Staff Ratio	1:1
Approximate Length	30 minutes
Therapeutic Rationale	To promote: • Deep breathing • Lung expansion
Precautions and Restrictions	This activity is not appropriate for asthmatic patients. Children participating must have the use of both hands and be ambulatory.
Required Skills	None
Equipment	Wooden blocks of various lengths Ping-pong ball Straw
Implementation	1. Assist the child in designing and constructing a maze out of the wooden blocks. 2. Place the ping-pong ball at one end of the maze. 3. Tell the child to use the straw to blow the ball through the maze. 4. Redesign and construct a new maze, increasing the difficulty if desired, and repeat steps 2 and 3.
Variations	Design and construct two identical mazes, and have two children or teams compete to see who can blow the ball through the maze fastest.

A C T I V I T Y 1 1 - 7	*PINWHEELS*
Age Group	5 through 8 years
Patient/Staff Ratio	5:1
Approximate Length	30 minutes
Therapeutic Rationale	To promote: • Lung expansion • Deep breathing
Precautions and Restrictions	Children participating in the activity need the use of both hands. Check precautions for markers. Children may need assistance with punching and fastening.
Required Skills	Cutting Pasting Tracing
Equipment	Heavy construction paper Markers or crayons Brads (brass paper fasteners) Straws Ruler Penny Scissors Hole punch
Implementation	1. Have the children cut the construction paper into a 1-foot square. 2. Using a ruler, draw two lines; one from the upper left corner to the lower right corner, the second from the upper right corner to the lower left corner. 3. Instruct the children to use the penny to trace a circle around the point in the center where the two lines cross. 4. Encourage the children to decorate the front and the back of the paper with markers or crayons. Do not obscure the lines or the circle. 5. Cut along the lines to the edge of the circle. There will now be four connected sections. 6. Carefully bend (don't fold) the right corner of each section into the center, and hold in place. 7. Punch a hole in the straw. 8. Push the brad through the four corners of the paper and through one end of the straw. 9. Fasten the brad by bending the tips. 10. Encourage the children to blow the pinwheel to make it spin.

A C T I V I T Y 1 1 - 8	*SAILBOAT BLOWING*

Age Group 4 through 10 years

Patient/Staff Ratio 5:1

Approximate Length 30 minutes

Therapeutic Rationale To promote:
- Lung expansion
- Deep breathing

Precautions and Restrictions Children participating in this activity must have the use of both hands.
Check glue and scissor precautions.

Required Skills Cutting
Pasting

Equipment Tongue depressors
Clay
Jar lid
Construction paper
Straws
Shallow pan filled with water
Scissors
Glue or tape

Implementation
1. Place a small wad of clay in the center of a jar lid.
2. Instruct the children to insert a tongue depressor into the clay, molding the clay around the end of the tongue depressor.
3. To form the sail, have the children cut out a small triangle from construction paper. Tape or glue the triangle to the tongue depressor.
4. Place the boats in a pan filled with water.
5. Have the children blow the boats around the water using straws.

Variation Make the sailboats from corks, toothpicks, and construction paper.
Divide the pan into sections, and have an America's Cup race.

A C T I V I T Y 1 1 - 9	*STRAW BLOW PAINTING*

Age Group	3 through 10 years
Patient/Staff Ratio	3:1
Approximate Length	15 minutes
Therapeutic Rationale	To promote: • Lung expansion • Deep breathing
Precautions and Restrictions	Make sure young children understand how to blow through the straw so they do not aspirate or ingest the paint. Let the child practice first with a mixture of water and food coloring. Check the tongue for coloring to ensure that the child is doing the activity correctly. Check marker precautions.
Required Skills	Blowing
Equipment	Thin tempera paint Heavy-weight paper Straws or 4-inch piece of IV tubing Crayons or markers
Implementation	1. Drip the paint onto a piece of paper. 2. Instruct the children to blow the paint around the paper using a straw or IV tubing. Some children may need to be told to blow gently. 3. When the paint has dried, encourage the children to add detail to the picture with paint and paint brushes, crayons, or markers.

A C T I V I T Y 1 1 - 1 0	*TUNED BOTTLE BLOWING*

Age Group	3 through 10 years
Patient/Staff Ratio	5:1
Approximate Length	30 minutes
Therapeutic Rationale	To promote: • Lung expansion • Deep breathing
Precautions and Restrictions	None
Required Skills	Blowing
Equipment	Empty bottles (eight, narrow-mouthed) Water
Implementation	1. Fill all the bottles with water, varying the amounts. Bottles with more water will have a higher tone. 2. Place the bottles in a row, starting with the bottle with the least amount of water and ending with the bottle containing the most water. 3. Have the child blow into the mouth of the bottles. 4. Children may compose original tunes or duplicate familiar simple tunes.
Variations	Fill bottles with juices or soft drinks and let children drink them after completing the activity. (NOTE: Children should drink only from bottles into which they have blown. Use only clean bottles that have not held toxic substances.)

ADDITIONAL IDEAS

- Have bubble gum blowing contests. Surgical hats may be necessary if your patients are very good bubble blowers.
- Dramatize the "Three Little Pigs" by having the children "huff and puff and b-l-o-w the house down."
- Have a pretend birthday party. Sing and whistle party tunes, use noise makers, and let the patients blow out the candles on a cake.
- Make an old fashion pea shooter out of a straw and shoot little wads of paper at specified targets. Or use the straw to suck up pieces of paper and transfer them from one container to another.
- Blow bubbles. Cut the bottom out of a paper cup and dip it in a basin filled with a solution of dish detergent and water. Or give the children two straws, the tip of one inside the other. Instruct the children to use the straw to blow into the basin to create "bubble mountains."
- Purchase harmonicas, recorders, or horns and encourage the children to make music.
- During dramatic play encourage the children to imitate sirens blowing, lions roaring, or Tarzan calling.
- Blow up paper bags and pop them.
- Create a table-top race track and have children use straws to blow "paper cars" around the track.

REFERENCES

Behrman, R. & Vaughn, V. (1987). *Nelson's textbook of pediatrics* (13th ed.). Philadelphia: W.B. Saunders.

Blazer, S., Navek, Y. & Friedman, A. (1980). Foreign body in the airway: A review of 200 cases. *American Journal of Diseases of Children, 134,* 168-171.

Bronniman, S. & Burrows, B. (1986). A prospective study of the natural history of asthma: Remission and relapse rates. *Chest, 90,* 480-484.

Carroll, P. (1987). The right way to do chest physiotherapy. *RN, 50* (5), 26-29.

Clough, P., Lindenauer, D., Hayes, M., & Zekany, B. (1986). Guidelines for routine respiratory care of patients with spinal cord injury, a clinical report. *Physical Therapy, 66* (9), 1395-1402.

Cosenza, J. & Celentano, N. (1986). Secretion clearance: State of the art from a nursing perspective. *Critical Care Nurse, 6* (4), 23-29.

Ellis, E. (1988). Asthma: Current therapeutic approach. *Pediatric Clinics of North America, 35* (5), 1041-1052.

Feeg, V. & Harbin, R. (1991). *Pediatric nursing: Care curriculum and research manual,* New Jersey: A. Jannetti Publications.

Hagedown, M., Gardner, S., & Abman, S. (1989). Respiratory disease. In G. Merenstein & S. Gardner (Eds.). *Handbook of neonatal intensive care,* (2nd ed.). St. Louis: Mosby–Year Book, Inc.

Kaluger, G. & Kaluger, M.F. (1984). *Human development: The span of life,* (3rd ed.). St. Louis: Mosby–Year Book, Inc.

Kendig, E.L. & Chernick, V. (1983). *Disorders of the respiratory tract in children,* (4th ed.). Philadelphia: W.B. Saunders.

LaMontagne, L.L. (1984). Three coping strategies used by school-age children. *Pediatric Nursing, 10* (1), 25-28.

Meyers, P. (1988). Parental adaptation to cystic fibrosis. *Journal Pediatric Health Care, 2,* 20-28.

Romero, R. (1986). Autobiographical scrapbooks: A coping tool for hospitalized school children. *Issues in Comprehensive Pediatric Nursing, 9,* 247-258.

Shaffer, D.R. (1985). *Developmental psychology: Theory, research and applications.* Monterey, CA: Brooks/Cole Publishing Co.

Tiep, B., Burns, M., Kao, D., Madison, R., & Herrera, J. (1986). Pursed lips breathing training using ear oximetry. *Chest, 90* (2), 218-221.

Whaley, L. & Wong, D. (1991). *Nursing care of infants and children* (4th ed.). St. Louis: Mosby–Year Book, Inc.

Whaley, L. & Wong, D. (1989). *Essentials of Pediatric Nursing* (3rd ed.). St. Louis: The C.V. Mosby Co.

Wohl, M. (1986). Bronchiolitis. *Annuals of Pediatrics, 15* (4), 307-313.

Zahr, L.K., Connolly, M., & Page, D.R. (1989). Assessment and management of the child with asthma. *Pediatric Nursing, 15* (2), 109-114.

CHAPTER 12

PERCEPTUAL-MOTOR ACTIVITIES

Fig. 12-1 Pincer pickup.

*I*n the United States, 10% to 15% of all children have a long-term physical disorder (Hobbs, Perrin, & Ireys, 1985). One percent of the total childhood population has an illness or disability that interferes with the child's participation in usual daily activities on a regular basis. Hearing impairment is the most common long-term handicapping disorder affecting children, whereas vision impairment is the fourth most common disability in the United States (Casper, 1985). Skeletal injuries and structural abnormalities are other conditions that may or may not result in long-term sequelae for children. A wide variety of childhood disabilities result in limiting perceptual-motor capabilities.

In this chapter information is provided so that individuals involved in planning therapeutic activities for children with perceptual-motor dysfunctions can develop effective plans for helping the child and family. Children with perceptual-motor disabilities or other chronic illnesses have the same needs and developmental concerns as children who are well. These are children who have hobbies, favorite sports teams, classes, and friends, but who also have cerebral palsy or vision or hearing impairments. Activities are suggested that support the individual child's level of perceptual-motor ability.

BACKGROUND INFORMATION

No matter what the diagnosis, the presence of a perceptual-motor disability imposes additional problems for the child and parents. Growing up presents difficult adjustment tasks for *all* children, and then the child must cope with the impact of a disability or serious injury that limits perceptual capabilities or mobility.

The impact of a perceptual-motor dysfunction on a child's social, emotional, and cognitive development differs considerably depending on the child's age at onset, the constraints caused by the condition at each phase of the child's development, the child's psychological resiliency, the natural history and prognosis of the illness, the necessity for physical care, and the degree to which the illness or disability is visible (Hobbs, Perrin, & Ireys, 1985). The emotional distress that accompanies a child's illness or disability extends to the rest of the family. Mothers, fathers, and siblings are subject to adjustment problems (Horner, Rawlins, & Giles, 1987). Studies have shown, however, that children with perceptual-motor dysfunctions and their families who receive care directed at mediating the stress and improving the outcome can meet these challenges (Barnard, 1987; Scipien, Chard, Howe, & Barnard, 1990).

A variety of sensory and motor experiences are needed to stimulate cognitive and psychosocial growth for a child. Normal sensorimotor play and exploration of the environment can be impossible for the child with perceptual-motor impairments. The inability to move about at will, to touch, to hear, or to feel can prevent the child from experiencing a sense of mastering and competence (Lee & Fowler, 1986; Foster, Hunsberger, & Anderson, 1989). In addition to affecting the child's physiologic well being, impaired sensory and motor systems can significantly affect the child's self-concept and attainment of developmental tasks. Mobility is essential to a child's ability to learn about the relationship between cause and effect, to develop independent skills, and to exert control over the environment (Breslau, Weitzman, & Messenger, 1981; Hobbs & Perrin, 1985; Whaley & Wong, 1991).

Children gain an understanding of the world

through the perception of events and communication of ideas and feelings. Dysfunctions that involve an alteration in perception or ability to communicate can interfere with successful development (Phillips & Hartley, 1988; Stark, 1989).

The child's ability to process sensory input is influenced by the level of functioning of the child's sensory organs. Much of the sensory data a child uses to interpret the world is visual and auditory. When the child has significant visual impairment or hearing loss, the amount of accessible information can alter his perception of the world surrounding him (Aram, 1987). Similarly, restraint of movement or diminished tactile sensation influences the child's perception and response to the environment (Hourcade & Parette, 1984; McCormick, Charney, & Stemmler, 1986).

The child who is developmentally delayed may exhibit difficulty processing information and performing age-appropriate skills. The child's developmental level is the best guide for selection of appropriate activities. Clear, simple directions and adequate supervision are necessary for activities involving the child with a developmental disability.

SPECIAL CONSIDERATIONS

A child with a deficit in motor skills may be at increased risk for accidental injury. Lack of motor control makes the child unable to protect himself against falling from a bed or chair. During activities the child must be positioned appropriately and postural supports used to maintain body alignment. If the child requires the use of a wheel chair, safety restraints must always be used. For the child with a seizure disorder, activities may be limited or a protective helmet may be necessary. Fears about risks associated with seizure disorders can result in the child being overprotected and the family expecting less of the child (Mott, James, & Sperhac, 1990).

Children who have skeletal dysfunctions or undergo orthopedic procedures may have enforced immobility during the treatment process. Restriction of movement, no matter what the rea-

son, is very frustrating for a child because children use movement as a coping strategy to reduce stress (Broome, 1986; Murphy & Moriarity, 1976; Savedra & Tesler, 1981).

ACTIVITY GOALS

Activities for the child with perceptual-motor dysfunction are directed toward accomplishing the following: (1) maximizing the child's perceptual and motor abilities; (2) enabling the child to learn methods of enhancing movement, control, and sensation; and (3) preventing complications associated with immobility or sensory impairment. The goal of activities should be to maximize the child's independence and freedom while providing safeguards from accidents. A child with perceptual-motor dysfunction or related illnesses may have decreased energy reserves. The child should be assessed for signs of fatigue. Attention span and interest in activities may be decreased. The activity plan must allow adequate rest periods for the child.

For the child with disabilities, modification of activities may be necessary. Finger painting may become toe painting. Visual cues and pictures may have to replace verbal communications. The child with a visual impairment must touch the physical boundaries of a room or play area to identify spatial relationships and points of reference (Nelson, 1984; Steffe, Suty, & Delcalzo, 1985).

The child's assistive devices may also necessitate modifying activities. Toys can be adapted with special controls so that the child can operate them. Play materials, games, and books can be stabilized to allow the child more independent manipulation.

Advances in electronic communication aids and computer-assisted educational equipment are providing new opportunities for the child with a perceptual-motor dysfunction to learn and be independent. It is important, however, that the electronic aids and computers are appropriate to the child's needs and capabilities so as not to lead to frustration and failure for the child.

ACTIVITY 12-5

HEAR AND DO GAME

Age Group

3 through 12 years

Patient/Staff Ratio

7:1

Approximate Length

20 minutes

Therapeutic Rationale

To increase concentration skills by:
• Following a sequence of directions in the order they are given

Precautions and Restrictions

None

Required Skills

None

Equipment

None

Implementation

1. If activity involves more than one player, divide players into two teams.
2. Have teams stand on opposite sides of the room facing each other.
3. Give the children a set of directions, its complexity determined by the players' abilities.
4. Call the names of one player from each team.
5. The two children called must follow the directions in the order in which they were given.
6. The first child to finish correctly and return to his or her place earns a point for his or her team.
7. Sample directions:
   Touch someone on the other team who is wearing blue; walk around the room three times; touch your hands to the floor.

Variation

This activity may be adapted to promote movement and exercise of specific body parts.

A C T I V I T Y 1 2 - 6	*IV BEDPAN TOSS*

Age Group	5 through 10 years
Patient/Staff Ratio	5:1
Approximate Length	20 minutes
Therapeutic Rationale	To develop eye-hand coordination by: • Tossing IV bags into buckets or bedpans
Precautions and Restrictions	This activity requires the use of one hand.
Required Skills	None
Equipment	IV bag filled with water Masking tape Bedpans
Implementation	1. Place a 1-foot piece of masking tape on the floor to designate where the children should stand when throwing the bag. 2. Arrange the bedpans in a vertical line in front of the masking tape leaving a 6-inch space between each bedpan. 3. The children should take turns throwing the IV bags into the bedpans, starting with the closest bucket and proceeding outward.
Variation	Use beanbags and buckets or bowls in place of IV bags and bedpans.

ACTIVITY 12-7   *MEMORY GAME*

Age Group	3 through 12 years
Patient/Staff Ratio	5:1
Approximate Length	20 minutes
Therapeutic Rationale	To increase concentration skills by: • Recalling objects on a tray after seeing them for only a few minutes
Precautions and Restrictions	None
Required Skills	None
Equipment	Assortment of small objects the child is familiar with Towel Paper Pen
Implementation	1. Make a list of all the objects. 2. Arrange the objects on a table within an area small enough to be covered by a towel. 3. Specify an amount of time the child may use to study the objects. 4. Allow the child to study the objects and then cover the objects with the towel. 5. Have the child write or dictate the names of all the objects he or she can remember. 6. As the child's ability increases, increase the number of objects accordingly.
Variation	Put several articles out and have the child close his or her eyes. Remove one or two articles; have the child open his or her eyes and name the article(s) removed. To make the game more difficult, rearrange the remaining articles before he or she looks again.

ACTIVITY 12-8

MILK BOTTLE DROP

Age Group	4 through 12 years
Patient/Staff Ratio	5:1
Approximate Length	20 minutes
Therapeutic Rationale	To improve eye-hand coordination by: • Dropping a clothes pin into a small-mouthed bottle
Precautions and Restrictions	None
Required Skills	None
Equipment	Clothes pins Small-mouth plastic bottle

Implementation

1. This activity may be done while sitting or standing.
2. Participants must drop the clothes pins into the bottle. A point is scored for each pin that lands in the bottle.
3. The game can be made more difficult by changing the position of the bottle.

A C T I V I T Y   1 2 - 9   *MIRROR ME*

Age Group	5 through 12 years
Patient/Staff Ratio	4:1
Approximate Length	15 minutes
Therapeutic Rationale	To increase concentration skills by: • Following movements of another person
Precautions and Restrictions	Must be determined on an individual basis.
Required Skills	None
Equipment	Record player Record
Implementation	1. Select a record with a smooth rhythm. 2. Instruct the children to follow the activity leader's movements as closely as possible. 3. The activity leader should perform simple movements that require movement of those body parts that are problematic for the child. 4. As the child becomes more adept, the complexity of the movements may be increased. 5. Children can be given the opportunity to lead the activity.

A C T I V I T Y   1 2 - 1 0   *MOBILE*

Age Group	Birth to 4 months
Patient/Staff Ratio	1:1
Approximate Length	30 minutes to make the mobile
Therapeutic Rationale	To provide visual stimulation by: • Watching figures on the mobile
Precautions and Restrictions	Do not use with infants at risk for overstimulation. Check with medical staff. Infants should not be allowed to touch construction paper; it can cut their fingers.
Required Skills	None
Equipment	Colored construction paper Butterfly pattern Hole punch Scissors String Cardboard Glue

Implementation

1. Trace and cut 5 large butterflies, 9 small butterflies, and 12 hearts (Fig. 12-2).
2. Cut two strips of cardboard 12 inches long and 3 inches wide and two pieces of string 20 inches long.
3. Staple two strips of cardboard into a circle and punch four sets of equidistant holes.
4. Thread one piece of string through a hole on the mobile, across the inside of the frame, and out through the opposite hole. Repeat, using the second piece of string.
5. Gather the ends together and tie all four ends of the string in a knot. This will create a mobile hanger.
6. Fold five of the small butterflies on the fold lines indicated on the pattern. Place a small amount of glue between the fold lines and glue to the larger butterflies.
7. Punch a hole in the center of the two butterflies and cut a small slit from the tail of the butterflies, almost to the hole.
8. Hold the butterflies with the small one on the bottom and the large one on top. Insert a string through the punched hole and tie it to the butterflies. The knot of the string should be on top of the large butterfly.
9. Carefully slip the string through the slit and adjust the butterfly so that it hangs horizontally.
10. Repeat this step with the remaining large butterflies.
11. Decorate the mobile with the remaining small butterflies and hearts.

Step 11

Fig. 12-2, cont'd

A C T I V I T Y 1 2 - 1 1	*PASTA PAINTING*
Age Group	3 years through 8 years
Patient/Staff Ratio	5:1
Approximate Length	20 minutes
Therapeutic Rationale	To provide tactile stimulation by: • Painting with the pasta mixture
Precautions and Restrictions	Patients must have the use of one hand. Children who are NPO should be well supervised to ensure none of the mixture is consumed.
Required Skills	None
Equipment	Fettucine, spaghetti, vermicelli, or other similar pasta Water Bowls Food coloring Cardboard or other heavy material to "paint" on Hot plate
Implementation	1. Cook the pasta according to package directions. Drain. 2. Determine how many different colors you wish to tint the pasta and divide the pasta into as many bowls. 3. Mix each bowl of pasta with the desired shade of food coloring. 4. Cover and refrigerate overnight. 5. Allow the children to use the pasta to "paint" on the cardboard or other heavy material. 6. Be sure to allow sufficient time for drying if the children wish to keep their artwork.

ACTIVITY 12-12	*PICTURE WEAVING*

Age Group	5 through 12 years
Patient/Staff Ratio	5:1
Approximate Length	20 to 30 minutes
Therapeutic Rationale	To develop eye-hand coordination by: • Weaving a picture
Precautions and Restrictions	Participants must have the use of one hand. Check glue precautions.
Required Skills	Pasting
Equipment	Full-page magazine illustration Construction paper Scissors Rubber cement
Implementation	1. Tell the children to fold the magazine picture in half. 2. Have them cut an odd number of equidistant slits extending from the fold and ending 1 inch from the edge of the paper. 3. Instruct the children to cut the construction paper into 1-inch strips. 4. Have them unfold the magazine illustration and weave them with the construction paper strips. 5. Trim any construction paper that extends beyond the edge of the magazine picture. 6. Use the rubber cement to affix the ends of the strips to the magazine illustration.

A C T I V I T Y 1 2 - 1 3	*PINCER PICK UP*

Age Group	12 through 36 months
Patient/Staff Ratio	1:1
Approximate Length	5 to 10 minutes
Therapeutic Rationale	To improve eye-hand coordination and pincer grasp by: • Picking up objects with thumb and fourth finger
Precautions and Restrictions	Children must be closely supervised to ensure they do not place objects in their mouths.
Required Skills	None
Equipment	A box with dividers 1-inch wide and no more than 2 inches tall; the height of the box should not exceed the length of the child's fingers Several high-interest objects, small enough to fit in the compartments of the box
Implementation	1. Place the objects into the compartments of the box. 2. Encourage the child to remove all of the objects from the compartments.

ACTIVITY 12-14   *PLAY SMOCKS*

Age Group	6 to 36 months
Patient/Staff Ratio	1:1
Approximate Length	10 to 15 minutes
Therapeutic Rationale	To develop eye-hand coordination by:

- Taking objects out of apron or smock pocket
- Putting objects in apron or smock pocket
- Opening and closing a zipper
- Buttoning and unbuttoning buttons

Precautions and Restrictions

A consistent caregiver should provide this activity.

Smocks must be washed after use with patients having a contagious disease.

Required Skills

Grasping

Equipment

Smock
Zipper
Buttons
Fabric
Needle
Thread

Implementation

1. The activity leader should sew extra pockets, buttons, and zippers to the front of the smock or apron.
2. During play time the activity leader should wear the play smock while interacting one-on-one with babies.
3. Encourage the baby to manipulate various things on the smock.

A C T I V I T Y 1 2 - 1 5	*SEWING CARDS*

Age Group	3 through 6 years
Patient/Staff Ratio	5:1
Approximate Length	15 minutes
Therapeutic Rationale	To improve eye-hand coordination by: • Lacing sewing cards
Precautions and Restrictions	Participants must have the use of one hand.
Required Skills	None
Equipment	Cardboard Scissors Hole punch Yarn tape Marker
Implementation	1. Before the activity, an adult should prepare the sewing cards. Draw various shapes on the cardboard. 2. Cut the shapes out. 3. Punch holes approximately ¾ inch apart around the edges of the shape. 4. Wrap one end of the yarn with tape to stiffen it. Tie a knot at the other end. 5. Have the children sew in and out of the holes.
Variation	Children can use plastic darning needles and yarn to create their own designs on squares of loosely woven fabric.

ACTIVITY 12-16

SIMON SAYS

Age Group 3 through 12 years

Patient/Staff Ratio 5:1

Approximate Length 15 minutes

Therapeutic Rationale To improve concentration skills by:
- Listening for commands accompanied by the words "Simon Says"
- Performing all commands accompanied by the words "Simon Says"

Precautions and Restrictions Certain restrictions may be imposed by the nature of a child's condition.

Required Skills None

Equipment None

Implementation
1. The players stand in a semicircle, except for "Simon" who stands in front of the others.
2. Simon starts the game by calling out a command such as "Simon says touch your toes." Players in the circle must follow the command.
3. If Simon omits the words "Simon says" and simply gives a command, the players must not carry out the command.
4. If a player makes a mistake, he or she becomes "Simon" and the game continues as before.

A C T I V I T Y 1 2 - 1 7	*TACTILE COLLAGE*
Age Group	3 through 12 years
Patient/Staff Ratio	5:1
Approximate Length	20 minutes
Therapeutic Rationale	To provide sensory and tactile stimulation by: • Using different textured materials to create a collage
Precautions and Restrictions	Participants must have the use of one hand.
Required Skills	None
Equipment	Clear contact paper Fabric scraps of assorted texture Yarn Pieces of sand paper Cotton puffs Masking tape
Implementation	1. Provide each child with a large piece of contact paper. 2. Tape the contact paper to the table with the adhesive facing up. 3. Have the children create a collage by placing the scrap materials on the adhesive. 4. Discuss the creation, emphasizing the different textures and shapes.

ACTIVITY 12-18	*TEXTURE BOOK*

Age Group	Birth to 24 months
Patient/Staff Ratio	1:1
Approximate Length	5 to 15 minutes
Therapeutic Rationale	To provide sensory and tactile stimulation by: • Touching fabrics of different textures • Looking at brightly colored fabrics
Precautions and Restrictions	Fabric squares must be changed for each child. Laminated cardboard should be disinfected between uses.
Required Skills	None
Equipment	Six 8-inch squares of brightly colored, different textured fabrics such as: Burlap Satin Luxury fur Flannel Corduroy Three laminated, 12 inch-squares of heavy cardboard Three metal binder rings One package of Velcro dots
Implementation	1. Cut the fabric and squares. 2. Laminate the cardboard squares. This can be done using clear plastic contact paper or at a professional laminating center. 3. If desired, finish the edges of the fabric squares. 4. Attach a Velcro dot to each corner of the fabric square. 5. With a pencil, lightly draw an 8-inch square on the laminated cardboard. 6. Attach a Velcro dot to each corner of the pencil square on the laminated cardboard. 7. Punch three holes in each of the laminated cardboard squares and insert the metal binder rings. 8. Attach the fabric to the cardboard. 9. Allow the child to look at the book. 10. Talk to the child about the different textures and have them describe how they feel. 11. When the child is finished, remove the fabric squares and disinfect the laminated cardboard. Fabric squares can be reused if they are disinfected.

A C T I V I T Y 1 2 - 1 9	*TEXTURE EXPERIENCES*
Age Group	Birth to 6 months
Patient/Staff Ratio	1:1
Approximate Length	5 to 10 minutes
Therapeutic Rationale	To provide sensory and tactile stimulation by: • Touching fabrics of different textures • Looking at brightly colored fabrics
Precautions and Restrictions	Materials that cannot be washed must only be used once to avoid transmitting infection. Materials that may be irritating to the skin should be avoided.
Required Skills	None
Equipment	Assorted swatches of textured materials such as: Burlap Corduroy Cotton Feathers Fur Satin Terrycloth Velvet
Implementation	1. Gently rub the baby's skin with the various textures. 2. Allow older infants to handle the materials.

ACTIVITY 12-20	*TUTTI-FRUTTI DOUGH*

Age Group	4 through 8 years
Patient/Staff Ratio	5:1
Approximate Length	30 minutes
Therapeutic Rationale	To provide olfactory and tactile stimulation by: • Touching the play dough • Identifying the smell of the play dough • Rolling out the play dough with hands and fingers
Precautions and Restrictions	Children must have the use of both hands. Although the mixture is nontoxic, consumption of the mixture should be avoided.
Required Skills	None
Equipment	Bowls (2) Spoon Powdered drink mix (two packages, preferably two different flavors) Flour (3 cups) Salt (1 cup) Water (approximately 1 cup) Tongue depressors Assorted cookie cutters
Implementation	1. Combine the flour, salt, and water in a bowl and mix well. 2. Divide the mixture into two equal portions. 3. Add one package powdered drink mix to each portion and mix well. 4. Have the children knead the mixture until it becomes soft and pliable. 5. Allow the children to use the cookie cutters, tongue depressors, or their hands to create various forms and shapes. While the children are playing with the mixture, encourage them to smell the aroma and identify the fruit flavor.

ADDITIONAL IDEAS

- To promote motor coordination, play follow the leader.
- To increase eye-foot coordination, play hopscotch. A removable hopscotch board can be made on the floor with masking tape.
- Design relay races that meet specific movement needs of patients.
- To promote finger and hand movement and control, use finger puppets or make shadow puppets.
- Sponsor a "Special Olympics" or carnival adapted to meet specific movement needs of the patients participating.

- Use dramatic play to encourage the movement of specific body parts. For example, have the children fly like Superman to promote movement and arm extension.
- Design an obstacle course for the playroom.
- Encourage fine motor development by providing art and craft activities.
- Offer "Hospital Aerobic" classes.
- Put an empty thread spool on a pencil to assist a child in grasping the pencil.
- Provide sandpaper for blind children to color.

REFERENCES

Aram, D. (1987). Disorders of hearing, speech, and language. In R.E. Behrman & V.C. Vaughn (Eds.), *Nelson's textbook of pediatrics*. (13th ed.). Philadelphia: W.B. Saunders.

Barnard, K.E. (1987). Forward. In M.H. Rose & R.B. Tomas (Eds.), *Children with chronic conditions: Nursing in a family and community context*. Orlando: Grune and Stratton.

Breslaut, N., Weitzman, M., & Messenger, K. (1981). Psychologic functioning of siblings of disabled children. *Pediatrics, 67* (3), 344-353.

Casper, J. (1985). Disorders of speech and voice. *Pediatric Annals, 14* (3), 220-229.

Foster, R.L.R., Hunsberger, M.M., & Anderson, J.J.T. (1989). *Family-centered nursing care of children*. Philadelphia: W.B. Saunders.

Hobbs, N. & Perrin, J.M. (1985). *Issues in the care of children with chronic illness*. San Francisco: Jossey-Bass, Inc.

Hobbs, N., Perrin, J.M., & Ireys, H.T. (1985). *Chronically ill children and their families*. San Francisco: Jossey-Bass, Inc.

Horner, M.M., Rawlins, P., & Giles, K. (1987). How parents of children with chronic conditions perceive their own needs. *MCN* (Jan/Feb), *12,* 40-43.

Hourcade, J. & Parette, H.P. (1984). Cerebral palsy and emotional disturbance: A review and implications for intervention. *Journal of Rehabilitation, 50,* 55-60.

Lee, J. & Fowler, M.D. (1986). Merely child's play? Developmental work and playthings. *Journal of Pediatric Nursing, 1* (4), 260-270.

McCormick, M.D., Charney, E.B., & Stemmler, M.M. (1986). Assessing the impact of a child with spina bifida on the family. *Developmental Medicine and Child Neurology, 28,* 53-61.

Mott, S.R., James, S.R., & Sperhac, A.M. (1990). *Nursing care of children and families* (2nd ed.). Menlo Park, California: Addison-Wesley.

Murphy, L. & Moriarity, A. (1976). *Vulnerability, coping and growth*. New Haven, Conn: Yale University Press.

Nelson, L.B. (1984). The visually handicapped child. *Pediatric Review, 6* (6), 173-182.

Philips, S. & Hartley, J.T. (1988). Developmental differences and interventions for blind children. *Pediatric Nursing,* May-June, 201-204.

Savedra, L. & Tesler, M. (1981). Description of the pain experience: A study of school-age children. *Issues in Comprehensive Pediatric Nursing, 5,* 373-380.

Scipien, G.M., Chard, M.A., Howe, J., & Barnard, M. (1990). *Pediatric nursing care,* St. Louis: Mosby–Year Book, Inc.

Stark, R.E. (1989). Early language intervention: When, why, how? *Infant-Young Children, 1* (4), 44-53.

Steffe, D.R., Suty, K.A., & Delcalzo, P.V. (1985). More than a touch: communicating with a blind and deaf patient. *Nursing, 15* (8), 36-39.

Whaley, L. & Wong, D. (1991). *Essentials of pediatric nursing* (4th ed.). St. Louis: Mosby–Year Book, Inc.

C H A P T E R

13

PAIN MANAGEMENT ACTIVITIES

Fig. 13-1 Magic bottle.

A c t i v i t i e s

lthough pain relief has been a central goal for the compassionate health care provider, until recently pain management, especially in children, was often an ignored aspect of care. Some of this undertreatment of pain may be related to the fact that the phenomenon of pain in children was not widely recognized until the 1970s (Schechter, Allen, & Hanson, 1986). Since that time numerous investigators have reported that inadequate pain relief is commonplace (Bonica, 1980; Eland, 1989; Keeri-Szanto & Heaman, 1972; Marks & Sachar, 1973; Mather & McKie, 1983) and that misconceptions regarding analgesic usage and addiction persist in members of the health care team (Cohen, 1980; Donovan et al, 1989; Schechter, Allen, & Hanson, 1986). Whereas the state of pain management has improved somewhat for adults, children's pain has received more limited attention and is treated less vigorously than that of adults. Therefore, health care providers who work with children will frequently encounter a child having unrelieved moderate-to-severe pain.

One of the most difficult problems impacting pain control has been the inability to accurately measure or assess pain intensity in children (Syrjala & Chapman, 1984; Ross & Ross, 1988). Because there have been no objective measures of pain, many clinicians have used informal methods of self-report and behavioral observations to obtain estimates of pain intensity in children (Beyer & Aradine, 1988). The difficulty in accurately assessing pain in children can contribute to the use of pain reduction strategies when the actual problem is fear or anxiety. On the other hand, fear- and anxiety-reducing strategies may be used when the major problem is pain. In this chapter information is provided so that individuals involved in planning therapeutic activities can develop a more individualized and effective plan for managing pain experienced by children and adolescents. Therapeutic activities vary in their effectiveness in helping the child cope with pain depending on factors such as age, gender, previous pain experiences, and parental presence (Broome, 1986). Recommendations of strategies for decreasing unnecessary pain and therapeutic activities for helping the child cope with pain are described.

BACKGROUND INFORMATION

Generally pain is defined in terms of physiological processes, protective mechanisms, perceptual phenomena, or subjective experiences. The International Association for the Study of Pain defines pain as "an unpleasant sensory and emotional experience associated with actual or potential tissue damage or described in terms of such damage" (Ross & Ross, 1988, p. 250).

Pain is not a simple stimulus-reflex response. Individual perceptions regarding the same painful event vary considerably. Factors within the child and between the child and individuals in his or her environment can influence a child's ability to deal with pain. The cognitive-developmental level of a child plays a crucial role in the child's perception and response to pain. Selection of therapeutic activities for pain management must be based on the child's level of development and maturity (Thompson & Varni, 1986).

Developmental Level: Implications for the Experience of Pain
Infant

Young infants respond to a painful stimulus with a generalized body response, usually accompanied by loud crying. Infants 6 months and older will begin to associate objects and individuals with pain and begin to cry before a painful procedure (Posnanski, 1978).

Intervention Activities for Infants

Soothing verbal reassurances
Rocking and holding of the infant
Pacifier for sucking
Providing a familiar cuddling object
Presence of parents

Toddler

The child from 1 to 3 years of age generally responds to pain in a resistive, combative, and verbally angry manner (Posnanski, 1976). A toddler is not able to conceptualize the rationale or the duration of the pain experience. The toddler learns about the world through sensorimotor mechanisms and uses activity to cope with painful experiences (Hester, 1979). Toddlers learn best by imitation of what is observed. Toddlers will often seek out a parent for comfort. Talking the toddler through a painful event can be an effective use of distraction.

Intervention Activities for Toddlers

Distraction by talking or listening to music
Video cartoons
Active play—allow the child to act out the events being experienced
Presence of parents

Preschool

The preschool-age child is limited in the ability to understand the cause of pain and may attribute causation to magic (Piaget & Inhelder, 1969). Preschool children cannot understand how a treatment that causes pain can also promote healing. They frequently use repetitive verbalization, such as "ouch, ouch, ouch" as distraction from pain. Recreating the pain experience during play can help a child at this age gain a sense of control.

Intervention Activities for Preschooler

Slow, rhythmic breathing or touch in the form of rubbing
Role play of painful experience
Distraction—singing a favorite song, or retelling a story
Repetitive verbalizations
Presence of parents

School Age

Several studies have documented that school-age children can describe the cause, type, quality, and quantity of pain (Savedra & Tesler, 1981; Abu-Sadd & Holzemer, 1981; Ross & Ross, 1988). Children of this age begin the concrete operational stage of thinking. They are able to use elementary logic and understand simple causal explanations (Piaget, 1969). School-age children are not usually physically resistive to a painful experience. In many instances they will attempt to gain control over the events by recalling previous painful experiences and successful coping behaviors. Ross and Ross (1988), in their study of 994 school-age children, found that 20% of the children in their sample identified their own coping strategies and that 20% identified relaxation, distraction, and fantasizing as their primary strate-

gies for coping with pain. Other studies of school-age children report the need for previous experience and practice with coping strategies to be effective (Tesler et al, 1981; Broome, 1985).

Intervention Activities for School-age Child

Distraction
Relaxation techniques
Preparation and rehearsal of painful experience

Adolescents

The child aged 12 and older is in the formal operation stage, is capable of abstract thought, understanding causality, problem solving, and appreciating relationships beyond the immediate experience (Piaget, 1969). This age group has the capacity to understand anxiety and fear of an experience (Steward & Steward, 1981).

Adolescents use many of the same pain-coping behaviors as school-age children. Intervention strategies include relaxation techniques, distraction imagery, and verbalization. In this age group the combination of imagery and a relaxation technique is very effective (Broome, 1985). Whatever coping strategies are selected for the adolescent, preparation and practice before the pain experience is important.

Intervention Activities for Adolescents

Verbalization
Imagery
Relaxation techniques
Pre-procedural preparation and practice

The ability to experience pain begins in infancy. Therefore, health care professionals must use a variety of strategies to assist the child to cope with pain. The intervention strategies should be based on the child's developmental level and promote the positive coping abilities of the child. During years of clinical experience, the following observations have been made related to pain management in children:

1. Children often deny pain because they fear needles.
2. Children's behavior response to pain is often misinterpreted as fear or loneliness.
3. Children receive inadequate doses of pain medications.

4. Children are capable of accurately reporting the amount of pain experienced.
5. Children know what activities are most effective in helping them cope with pain.

Surprisingly, clinicians have not reported using the parent as either a source of information or as an active intervenor in the management of children's pain (Broome & Lillis, 1989). Yet children identify their parents as the most important source of comfort when in pain (Broome & Slack, 1990; Ross & Ross, 1988). The parent-child relationship could be a significant factor in helping a child cope with a painful experience. Parents participate in many aspects of a child's hospitalization, and health care providers need to consider broadening parent participation in pain management. Perhaps the combination of health care professionals using the most current methods of pain control, such as PCA pumps, in conjunction with increased parent involvement, would enable pediatric caregivers to advocate in the best interests of the child.

SPECIAL CONSIDERATIONS

One of the most effective strategies children use to cope with stressful experiences, such as pain, is play. Therapeutic play has been widely used as a method of preparing children for hospitalization and surgery (Bates & Broome, 1986). Sigmund Freud (1961) considered play to be the vehicle whereby traumatic psychological events could be repetitively enacted, with the end result of the child feeling in control. For children, the loss of control is manifest in every aspect of their hospital experience. Therefore, the child should be given the opportunity to play, using appropriate equipment to facilitate his or her feeling of control (Young & Fu, 1988). According to Melzack and Wall (1982), both anxiety and pain seem to decrease with the acquisition of a sense of control. Other strategies that can be used to help children cope with stressful experiences include biofeedback, relaxation training, film modeling, and distraction.

Biofeedback

Biofeedback has been demonstrated to be an effective pain management intervention for children who have little difficulty in gaining volun-

tary control of a target response system. The limitations of biofeedback are that it requires sensitive electronic equipment and highly skilled, trained technicians to teach the child specific muscle relaxation techniques.

Relaxation Training

In contrast to biofeedback, relaxation techniques can be employed with simplicity and are less costly. The ability to relax is a valuable skill for a child who must undergo a painful treatment or experience unexpected pain. Ross and Ross (1984) report that some children seem to have acquired an ability to relax on their own. Relaxation can be accomplished through concentration on muscle groups, techniques of breathing, meditation, and conditioning processes. Generally for an infant or young child, rhythmic rocking and softly repeating one or two words are relaxing. For the older child progressive relaxation, letting body parts go limp, or slow, deep breathing are effective relaxation techniques (Broome, 1985; Whaley & Wong, 1991). The individual who wishes to teach children to relax should refer to clinicians or therapists who have established training procedures. Programs for teaching relaxation techniques have been developed by Cautela and Groden (1978) and Richter, McGrath, Humphreys, Goodman, Firestone, and Keene (1986).

Film Modeling

Film modeling is the use of films that portray models having a perceived similarity to the observer (same age, sex, and race) demonstrating a pattern of response behavior that reduces the child's fear of a painful situation. The model initially exhibits fear in the stress situation but overcomes it and demonstrates an ability to cope with pain (Melamed & Siegal, 1975; Elkins & Roberts, 1985).

Film model presentations have also been used with nonhospitalized children in classroom settings to increase the child's medical knowledge and improve his or her attitude (Elkins & Roberts, 1985; Ross & Ross, 1988). Research on the use of film modeling can be summarized as follows:

1. Children undergoing a painful procedure for the first time generally benefit, while

children with prior experience benefit less (Klinzing & Klinzing, 1977; Melamed, Dearborn, & Hermecz, 1983).

2. More fearful children decrease their fear level to a greater extent than the less fearful children (Elkins & Roberts, 1985).

3. Older children demonstrate significantly more increase in knowledge from pre-procedural preparation than younger children (Elkins & Roberts, 1985; Gilbert et al, 1982).

Distraction

The specific type of distraction employed depends on the age of the child, but the purpose is to divert the child's attention from a threatening procedure or a distressing situation. Most children want to participate in their care and readily become involved when asked to do something. Slow, rhythmic breathing or a specific pattern of breathing is an easy distraction technique to use with children. The child is instructed to take a deep breath through the nose and blow it out through the mouth. When the child makes a conscious effort to count the respirations, attention is focused on the breathing. Playing music, storytelling, talking about favorite places, or watching a video or television are effective distraction methods with children.

A C T I V I T Y 1 3 - 1	*COMEDY CART*

Age Group	4 years through adolescence
Patient/Staff Ratio	1:1
Approximate Length	5 minutes (to help child make selections)
Therapeutic Rationale	To reduce children's pain through: • Humorous distraction
Precautions and Restrictions	Do not use tapes or comic books that depict violence of any sort, such as The Three Stooges.
Required Skills	Reading, if reading material is selected.
Equipment	*Audiovideo* Stereos, tape players, or VCRs as needed Cart (a three-shelved book cart works well) Videotaped comedies and/or cartoons Audio tapes of funny songs or comedy albums *Other* Comic books Joke books Toys that make children laugh (e.g., a battery-operated bear that rollerskates, has a blinking nose, and plays music simultaneously)
Implementation	1. Decorate the cart to make it colorful and amusing. Contact paper of assorted bright colors and large, humorous cartoon characters can achieve this effect. Be sure not to make the cart look childish or it may not appeal to adolescents. 2. Place materials on the cart in an appealing fashion. 3. Allow the children to select items that interest them. 4. Have the children use the activities during periods of pain and/or stress.

ACTIVITY 13-2	*IMAGERY SCRAPBOOK*
Age Group	8 years through adolescence
Patient/Staff Ratio	1:1 (Scrapbooks may be constructed in a group situation, but support during painful situations should be 1:1.)
Approximate Length	Situational
Therapeutic Rationale	To reduce children's pain through: • Use of mental imagery to diminish anxiety by creating a pleasant imaginary environment
Precautions and Restrictions	A child needs to practice the use of mental imagery before a painful experience to use this technique successfully.
Required Skills	Cutting Writing
Equipment	Paper Assortment of old National Geographics, travel magazines, and travel brochures Inexpensive photo albums (preglued) Scissors Pen
Implementation	1. Have the children select pictures of places they find pleasant and relaxing. 2. Cut the pictures out and place them in the scrapbooks. 3. Have the children write short descriptions of what they like about the places in the pictures, what it would smell like, how they would feel if they were there, what they might hear, or what they would be doing. Place the descriptions under each picture. 4. When the child is under stress or in pain, use the imagery book to help the child imagine himself or herself in the appealing environments depicted in the book.

A C T I V I T Y   1 3 - 3   *LAST NIGHT FOR DINNER I HAD . . .*

Age Group   7 through 12 years

Patient/Staff Ratio   1:1 (Can be played with more players in unusual settings where groups of children who are experiencing pain or discomfort may be found, e.g., oncology clinics.)

Approximate Length   10 to 15 minutes

Therapeutic Rationale   To reduce child's pain through:
- Distraction using cognitive games

Precautions and Restrictions   None

Required Skills   Knowledge of the alphabet and its sounds

Equipment   None

Implementation
1. The game begins with the first player stating, "Last night for dinner I had . . . (player must name something beginning with the letter "a" such as avocado, apple pie, or artichokes).
2. The second player repeats the phrase, "Last night for dinner I had . . .," and must then name any foods named by the previous players and add a food beginning with the next consecutive letter of the alphabet.
3. Play continues through each letter of the alphabet in this manner. The letter "x" may need to be omitted because of a lack of food items beginning with this letter.

Variation   The game can be varied by using categories other than food. For example, "Yesterday at the zoo I saw . . . (players go through the alphabet inserting the names of animals).

A C T I V I T Y 1 3 - 4	*MAGIC BOTTLES*

Age Group	4 years through adolescence
Patient/Staff Ratio	1:1 (Bottles can be made during a group activity, if desired. However, support during painful situations should be 1:1.)
Approximate Length	10 minutes (to make the bottle)
Therapeutic Rationale	To reduce children's pain through: • Provision of a soothing visual distraction
Precautions and Restrictions	Child must have the use of one hand. Check glitter precautions.
Required Skills	None
Equipment	Empty, clean 1 liter plastic soda pop bottles (labels removed) Mineral oil Water Funnel Duct tape Glitter Sequins Food coloring (optional)
Implementation	1. Have the child put the funnel in the mouth of the bottle and fill the bottle halfway with mineral oil. 2. With the funnel still in the bottle opening, add desired amount of glitter and sequins. 3. Add water to within ½ inch from the top of the bottle. If desired, add a few drops of food coloring. 4. Place top on the bottle. Make sure it is on tightly. Secure the top with duct tape. 5. When the child has a period of acute pain or stress, gently shake the bottle and encourage the child to visually focus on the movement of the designs. 6. Young children may respond to the suggestion that the bottle is magic and it will help make the pain go away.

A C T I V I T Y 1 3 - 5	*MUSCLE RELAXATION EXERCISE*

Age Group	5 years through adolescence
Patient/Staff Ratio	1:1
Approximate Length	15 minutes
Therapeutic Rationale	To reduce pain by: • Promoting relaxation and a feeling of self-control
Precautions and Restrictions	Children need to practice this skill before the painful experience.
Required Skills	Listening and cognitive ability
Equipment	Rag doll
Implementation	1. Explain to the children that they will be learning about muscles: how to make them work and how to make them rest. Children should be instructed to think about their muscles and nothing else. 2. Have the children make a muscle in their left arm. Discuss how their left arm feels compared to their right arm. Have them relax their arm. Repeat the exercise, focusing on the right arm. 3. Instruct the children to flex their left foot. Discuss how their left leg feels compared to their right leg. Have them slowly relax their left leg. Repeat the exercise, focusing on the right leg. 4. Instruct the children to lie flat on the floor and stiffen their entire body. Arms should be above their heads and toes should be pointed. 5. Show the group the rag doll. Tell them to release their muscles so they are as limp as the doll. Allow the children to relax for 3 to 5 minutes.

ACTIVITY 13-6	*MUSIC TAPES*

Age Group

8 years through adolescence★

Patient/Staff Ratio

1:1

Approximate Length

Situational—because this activity is very time-consuming, it is suggested that parents or volunteers assist the child in selecting and recording the music.

Therapeutic Rationale

To reduce children's pain through:
 • The use of music to promote relaxation and provide distraction.

Precautions and Restrictions

None

Required Skills

None

Equipment

Extensive assortment of record albums, audio tapes, and/or compact discs
Stereo, tape player, and/or compact disc player
Tape recorder

Implementation

1. Explain to the child that music helps one relax and feel better when pain or stress is experienced.
2. Discuss what type of music makes the child feel good, e.g., lively marches, soothing classical.
3. Have the child listen to various music selections in the style he or she prefers and select personal favorites.
4. Create an audio tape of the child's favorites.
5. Play the tape when the child is experiencing pain.

★Parents can make tapes for younger children, selecting music they have observed their children respond to positively. Even small infants can benefit from soothing music when they are in pain.

ACTIVITY 13-7　*SQUEEZE AND LOOK BAGS*

Age Group　6 months through 2 years

Patient/Staff Ratio　1:1

Approximate Length　Situational

Therapeutic Rationale　To reduce children's pain through:
  • Visual distraction

Precautions and Restrictions　Children must be closely supervised to prevent them from mouthing or biting on the bag.

Required Skills　None

Equipment　Vacuum food-sealing machine and specially made bags (can be purchased at Sears, Roebuck, and Co.)
Assorted fillings such as:
colored sand
glitter
pieces of sponge saturated with liquid soap
mineral oil with a drop or two of food coloring

Implementation
1. Cut the bags to the desired size (3″ × 3″ works well).
2. Fill each bag with a different material or combination of materials. When using soapy pieces of sponge, fill the bag about half full with water.
3. Seal the bags according to the instructions that accompany the sealing machine.
4. Encourage the young child to manipulate and watch the bags when they are in pain or undergoing procedures.

ACTIVITY 13-8	*SUPER BUBBLES*

Age Group	3 through 8 years
Patient/Staff Ratio	1:1
Approximate Length	Situational
Therapeutic Rationale	To reduce children's pain through: • Provision of a visual and physical distraction • Promoting relaxation through breathing
Precautions and Restrictions	Be sure to use a coated wire hanger to ensure no sharp areas are exposed.
Required Skills	Blowing
Equipment	Liquid dishwashing soap (Dawn© works well) Glycerin (can be purchased at drug stores) or corn syrup Water (distilled water will produce longer lasting solutions) Soft wire or bendable coat hanger Shallow pan Bowl
Implementation	1. Make the bubble solution by combining 1 part detergent, 9 parts water, and ½ part glycerine or corn syrup. 2. Use the hanger or wire to make the wand. (Empty spools or paper cups with the bottom cut out work well, too.) 3. Initiate bubble blowing when the child is in acute pain or stress. Some children respond well to the imagery of "blowing the hurt away." 4. If necessary, model optimal breathing technique, i.e., slow, evenly paced breaths.

ACTIVITY 13-9	*TURKEY SPELL*

Age Group	8 years through adolescence
Patient/Staff Ratio	1:1 (or with several children)
Approximate Length	5 to 10 minutes
Therapeutic Rationale	To reduce children's pain through: • The use of cognitive games as distraction
Precautions and Restrictions	None
Required Skills	Spelling
Equipment	Dictionary
Implementation	1. The object of the game is to spell words, while using strategy so that the word will not be completed on your turn. When a word is completed on a player's turn, that person gets one letter from the word "turkey" (letters are given out consecutively to each player as they lose a round). The first player to receive all the letters in the word "turkey" loses the game. 2. Play begins by the first player thinking of a word and supplying the first letter. Players alternate giving letters until a word has been spelled; the player on who's turn the word is completed loses the round. For example, the first player says "t." The next player says "r," and the next player says "e." If the next player said "e," he or she would spell "tree" and lose the round. If that player had said "a," play would continue until a word had been spelled. 3. At any point during the game, a player who has just given a letter may be challenged by another player to say aloud the word being spelled. If there is no such word, the player being challenged would get a letter from the word "turkey" and lose the round. If the word is indeed valid, the challenger loses the round and receives a letter from "turkey." A dictionary should be consulted when there is a dispute.

ADDITIONAL IDEAS

- Use commercially available "sleep machines" that play repetitive sounds such as soft rain or lapping waves.
- Provide a young child with a cloth doll or soft stuffed animal to cuddle during painful procedures.
- Provide child with "Nintendo"® or other similarly engrossing video game to serve as a distraction from pain.
- Suggest simple attention-diverting strategies for the child to use during painful procedures, such as singing a song or counting backwards from 100.
- Provide the child with a commercially available "magic wand" (acrylic tubes filled with oil and glitter) to use as distraction. Young children may respond to the suggestion that the magic wand will help lessen the pain.
- Give the child an unfamiliar, interesting new toy to play with during a procedure. However, be sure this won't interfere with the procedure.
- Use pop-up books as a distraction.

REFERENCES

Abu-Sadd, H. & Holzemer, W.L. (1981). Measuring children's self-assessment of pain. *Issues in Comprehensive Pediatric Nursing, 5,* 337-349.

Bates, T. & Broome, M.E. (1986). Preparation of children for hospitalization and surgery: A review of the literature. *Journal of Pediatric Nursing, 1* (4), 230-239.

Beyer, J.E. & Aradine, C.R. (1988). Convergent and discriminate validity of a self-report measure of pain intensity for children. *Child Health Care* (Spring), 16 (4), 274-281.

Bonica, J.J. (1980). Pain research and therapy: Past and current status and future needs. In L.K.Y. Ng and J.J. Bonica (Eds.), *Pain, discomfort and humanitarian care.* New York: Elsevier/North-Holland, 1-46.

Broome, M.E. (1985). The child in pain: A model for assessment and intervention. *Critical Care Quarterly, 8,* 47-55.

Broome, M.E. (1986). The relationship between children's fears and behavior during a painful event. *Child Health Care* (Winter), *14* (3), 142-145.

Broome, M.E. & Lillis, P. (1989). A descriptive analysis of pediatric pain management research. *Applied Nursing Research* 74-85.

Broome, M.E. & Slack J.F. (1990). Influences on nurses' management of pain in children. *MCN, 15,* 158-162.

Cautela, J. & Groden, J. (1978). *Relaxation: A comprehensive manual for adults, children and children with special needs.* Champaign, Il: Research Press.

Cohen, F.L. (1980). Post-surgical pain relief: Patients' status and nurses' medication choices. *Pain, 9,* 265-274.

Donovan, M., Slack, J., Faut, M., & Wright, S. (1989). Factors associated with inadequate management of pain. *American Pain Society,* Eighth Annual Scientific Meeting, Phoenix.

Eland, J. (1989). Pharmacologic management of acute and chronic pediatric pain. *Issues Comprehensive Pediatric Nursing, 11,* 93-111.

Elkins, P.D. & Roberts, M.C. (1985). Reducing medical fears in a general population of children: A comparison of three audiovisual modeling procedures. *Journal of Pediatric Psychology, 10,* 65-75.

Freud, S. (1961). Beyond the pleasure principle. J. Strachey (Ed.), New York: W.W. Norton & Co., Inc.

Gilbert, B.O., Johnson, S.B., Spillar, R., McCalburn, M., Silverstein, J.H., & Rosenbloom, A. (1982). The effects of peer-modeling film on children learning to self-inject insulin. *Behavior Therapy, 13,* 186-193.

Hester, N.K. (1979). The preoperational child's reaction to immunization. *Nursing Research, 28,* 250-255.

Keeri-Szanto & Heaman, S. (1972). Postoperative demand analgesia. *Surgery, Gynecology and Obstetrics, 134,* 647-651.

Klinzing, D.R. & Klinzing, D.G. (1977). Communicating with young children about hospitalization. *Communication Education, 26,* 307-313.

Marks, R. & Sachar, E. (1973). Undertreatment of medical inpatients with narcotic analgesia. *Annals of Internal Medicine, 78,* 173-181.

Mather, L. & McKie, J. (1983). The incidence of postoperative pain in children. *Pain, 15,* 271-282.

Melamed, B.G. & Siegal, L.J. (1975). Reduction of anxiety in children facing hospitalization and surgery by use of film modeling. *Journal of Counseling and Clinical Psychology, 43,* 511-521.

Melamed, B.G., Dearborn, M., & Hermecz, D.A. (1983). Necessary considerations for surgery preparation: Age and previous experience. *Psychosomatic Medicine, 45,* 517-525.

Melzack, R. & Wall, P.D. (1982). *The challenge of pain.* New York: Basic Books.

Piaget, J. (1962). *Play and imitation in children.* New York: W.W. Norton & Co., Inc.

Piaget, J. & Inhelder, B. (1969). *The psychology of the child.* New York: Basic Books.

Posnanski, E.O. (1976). Children's reaction to pain: A psychiatrist's perspective. *Clinical Pediatrics, 15,* 1114-1119.

Richter, F., McGrath, P., Humphreys, P., Goodman, J., Firestone, P., & Keene, D. (1986). Cognitive and relaxation treatment of pediatric migrane. *Pain, 25,* 195-203.

Ross, D.M. & Ross, S.A. (1984). Stress reduction procedures for the school-age hospitalized leukemic child. *Pediatric Nursing, 10,* 393.

Ross, D.M. & Ross, S.A. (1988). Assessment of pediatric pain: An overview. *Issues Comprehensive Pediatric Nursing, 11,* (2-3), 73-91.

Ross, D.M. & Ross, S.A. (1988). *Childhood pain: current issues, research and management.* Baltimore, MD: Urban & Schwarzenberg, Inc.

Savedra, M. & Tesler, M. (1981). Coping strategies of hospitalized school-age children. *Western Journal of Nursing Research, 3* (4), 371-384.

Schechter, N.L., Allen, D.A., & Hanson, K. (1986). Status of pediatric pain control: A comparison of hospital analgesic usage in children and adults. *Pediatrics, 77,* 11-15.

Steward, M. & Steward, D. (1981). Children's conceptions of medical procedures. In R. Bibace & M. Walsh (Eds.), *Children's conceptions of health, illness and bodily functions.* San Francisco: Jossey-Bass, Inc.

Syrjala, K.L. & Chapman, C.R. (1984). Measurement of clinical pain: A review and integration of research findings. In C. Bennedetti, C.R. Chapman, & E. Moricca (Eds.), *Advances in pain research and therapy,* Vol. 7. New York: Raven Press.

Tesler, M., Wegner, C., Savedra, M., & Ward, J. (1981). Coping strategies of children in pain. *Issues in Comprehensive Pediatrics, 5,* 373-380.

Thompson, K.L. & Varni, J.W. (1986). A developmental cognitive-biobehavioral approach to pediatric pain assessment. *Pain, 25,* 283-296.

Whaley, L. & Wong, D. (1991). *Nursing Care of Infants and Children* (4th ed.). St. Louis: Mosby–Year Book, Inc.

Young, M.R. & Fu, V.R. (1988). Influence of play and temperament on the young child's response to pain. *CHC* (Winter), *16* (3), 209-215.

INDEX

DATE DUE